classic puddings & pies

classic puddings & pies

TRADITIONAL RECIPES FOR DELECTABLE DESSERTS

MARTHA DAY

LORENZ BOOKS

This edition published by Lorenz Books in 2001

© Anness Publishing Limited 1995, 2001

Published in the USA by Lorenz Books
Anness Publishing Inc.
27 West 20th Street
New York
NY 10011

Lorenz Books is an imprint of Anness Publishing Inc.

www.lorenzbooks.com

All rights reserved. No part of this publication may be reproduced, stored in a retrieval system, or transmitted in any way or by any means, electronic, mechanical, photocopying, recording or otherwise, without the prior written permission of the copyright holder.

Publisher: Joanna Lorenz
Editor: Linda Fraser
Designers: Tony Paine and Roy Prescott
Photographers: Steve Baxter, Karl Adamson and Amanda Heywood
Food for Photography: Wendy Lee, Jane Stevenson and Elizabeth Wolf-Choen

Front cover: William Lingwood, Photographer;
Helen Trent, Props Stylist; Sunil Vijayakar, Food Stylist

Previously published as *Creative Cooking Library: Traditional Puddings & Pies*

1 3 5 7 9 10 8 6 4 2

CONTENTS

Introduction *6*

Hot Desserts *10*

Cold Desserts *26*

Pies and Tarts *54*

Fruit Desserts *74*

Index *96*

INTRODUCTION

Home-made desserts, pies and tarts are a pleasure to make and delicious to eat. There are recipes here for every occasion throughout the year – you'll find puddings suitable for special celebrations and family meals, too. When you are planning a meal, the choice of the other courses is important; for instance, you might choose a light main course to go with a rich creamy dessert or a sweet and filling pie, or pick something hearty to go with one of the simpler, fruit desserts. If you are planning a festive meal or a party, make sure you leave plenty of time for preparation – and do some of the work ahead of time if you can. Pastry, for instance, can be made a day or two in advance and chilled until ready to use, or even frozen for up to 3 months if you are really organized! All the recipes have step-by-step instructions, and in this section you'll find special tips and techniques to help you make perfect egg custard, simple meringue and fruit sauces, as well as helpful hints on preparing the pastry and decorations for pies and tarts.

MAKING CUSTARD

A home-made custard is a luscious sauce for many hot and cold puddings. The secret for success is patience. Don't try to hurry the cooking of the custard by raising the heat.

Makes about 2 cups
2 cups milk
1 vanilla pod, split in half
4 egg yolks
3–4 tbsp caster sugar, to sprinkle

1 Put the milk in a heavy-based saucepan. Hold the vanilla pod over the pan and scrape out the tiny black seeds into the milk. Add the split pod to the milk.

2 Heat the milk gently until bubbles appear round the edge. Remove from the heat, cover and set aside to infuse for 10 minutes. Remove the split vanilla pod.

3 In a bowl, lightly beat the egg yolks with the sugar until smoothly blended and creamy. Gradually add the hot milk to the egg yolks, stirring constantly.

4 Pour the mixture into the top of a double saucepan (or a bowl). Set over the bottom pan containing hot water. Put on a moderately low heat, so the water stays below a boil.

5 Cook, stirring constantly, for 10–12 minutes or until the custard thickens to a creamy consistency that coats the spoon. Immediately remove the pan of custard from over the pan of hot water.

6 Strain the custard into a bowl. If using cold, sprinkle a little sugar over the surface of the custard to help prevent a skin from forming. Set the bowl in a container of iced water and leave to cool.

VARIATIONS
- Use 1 tsp vanilla extract instead of the vanilla pod. Omit steps 1 and 2, and add the extract after straining the custard.
- For Chocolate Custard add 2oz semi-sweet chocolate, grated, to the hot milk and sugar mixture. Stir until smooth before adding to the egg yolks.

DAMAGE REPAIR

If the custard gets too hot and starts to curdle, remove it from the heat immediately and pour it into a bowl. Whisk vigorously for 2–3 seconds or until smooth. Then pour it back into the pan and continue cooking.

MAKING A BERRY SAUCE

A smooth, uncooked berry sauce, called a 'coulis' in French, has a refreshing flavor and beautiful color. You can use fresh or frozen fruit for the sauce. If using frozen fruit, partially thaw and drain on kitchen paper before puréeing.

Makes about 1 cup

1lb raspberries, strawberries or blackberries
1–2oz confectioner's sugar, sifted
squeeze of lemon juice (optional)
1–2 tbsp Kirsch or fruit liqueur (optional)

1 Hull the berries if necessary. Put them in a bowl of cold water and swirl them round briefly. Scoop out and spread on paper towels. Pat dry. Purée the berries in a blender or food processor. Turn the machine on and off a few times and scrape down the bowl to be sure all the berries are evenly puréed.

2 For raspberries, blackberries and other berries with small seeds, press the purée through a fine-mesh nylon strainer. Add confectioner's sugar to taste, plus a little lemon juice and/or liqueur, if using (for example, choose raspberry liqueur, or *framboise*, if making a raspberry sauce). Stir well to dissolve the sugar completely.

MAKING SIMPLE MERINGUE

This soft meringue is used as a topping for pies. Take care when separating the egg whites and yolks because even the smallest trace of yolk will prevent the whites from being whisked to their maximum volume. All equipment must be clean and free of grease.

1 Put the egg whites in a large, clean and grease-free bowl. With a whisk or electric mixer, whisk the whites until they are foamy.

2 Continue whisking until the whites hold soft peaks when you lift the whisk or beaters (the tips of the peaks will flop over).

3 Sprinkle the sugar over the whites, whisking constantly. Continue whisking for about 1 minute or until the meringue is glossy and holds stiff peaks when you lift the whisk or beaters. The meringue is now ready to be spread on a pie filling.

SEPARATING EGGS

It is easier to separate the yolks and whites if eggs are cold. Tap the egg once or twice against the rim of a small bowl to crack the shell. Break open the shell and hold half in each hand. Carefully transfer the unbroken yolk from one half shell to the other several times, letting the egg white dribble into the bowl. Put the yolk in a second bowl.

4 Separate eggs carefully, making sure that there is no trace of egg yolk in the whites. (It is best to separate 1 egg at a time and check each white before adding it to the rest.)

COOK'S TIP

Egg whites can be whisked to their greatest volume if they are at room temperature rather than cold. A copper bowl and wire balloon whisk are the best tools to use, although a stainless steel or glass bowl and electric mixer also produce very good results.

PASTRY TIPS AND TECHNIQUES

ROLLING OUT AND LINING A PAN

A neat pie shell that doesn't distort or shrink in baking is the desired result. The key to success is handling the dough gently. Use the method here for lining a round pie or tart pan that is about 2in deep.

Remove the chilled dough from the refrigerator and allow it to soften slightly at room temperature. Unwrap and put it on a lightly floured surface. Flatten the dough into a neat round. Lightly flour the rolling pin.

1 Using even pressure, start rolling out the dough, working from the center to the edge each time and easing the pressure slightly as you reach the edge of the round.

2 Lift up the dough and give it a quarter turn from time to time during the rolling. This will prevent the dough sticking to the surface, and will help keep the thickness even.

3 Continue rolling out until the dough round is about 2in larger all round than the pan. The dough should be about ⅛in thick.

4 Set the rolling pin on the dough, near one side of the round. Fold the outside edge of dough over the pin, then roll the rolling pin over the dough to wrap the dough round it. Do this gently and loosely.

5 Hold the rolling pin over the pan and gently unroll the dough so it drapes into the pan, centering it as much as possible.

6 With your fingertips, lift and ease the dough into the pan, gently pressing it over the bottom and up the side. Turn excess dough over the rim and trim it with a knife or scissors, depending on the edge to be made.

COOK'S TIPS

● Reflour the surface and rolling pin if the dough starts to stick.

● Should the dough tear, patch with a piece of moistened dough.

● When rolling out and lining the pie or tart pan, do not stretch the dough. It will only shrink back during baking, spoiling the shape of the pie shell.

● During rolling out, gently push in the edges of the dough with your cupped palms, to keep the round shape.

● A pastry scraper will help lift the dough from the work surface, to wrap it around the rolling pin.

● When finishing the edge, be sure to hook the dough over the rim all the way round or to press the dough firmly to the rim. This will prevent the dough pulling away should it start to shrink.

● Pans made from heat-resistant glass or dull-finish metal such as heavyweight aluminum will give a crisp crust.

Making a Pie Shell

1 **For a forked edge**: trim the dough even with the rim and press it flat. Firmly and evenly press the prongs of a fork all round the edge. If the fork sticks, dip it in flour.

2 **For a crimped edge**: trim the dough to leave an overhang of about ½in all round. Fold the extra dough under. Put the knuckle or tip of the index finger of one of your hands inside the edge, pointing directly out. With the thumb and index finger of your other hand, pinch the dough edge around your index finger into a 'V' shape. Continue all round the edge.

3 **For a cut-out edge**: trim the dough even with the rim and press it flat on the rim. With a small cookie cutter, cut out decorative shapes from the dough trimmings. Moisten the edge of the pie shell and press the cutouts in place, overlapping them slightly if you like.

Making a Two-crust Pie

1 Roll out half of the pastry dough on a floured surface and line a pie pan that is about 2in deep. Trim the dough even with the rim.

3 Trim the edge of the lid to leave a ½in overhang. Cut slits or a design in the center. These will act as steam vents during baking.

2 Roll out a second piece of dough to a circle that is about 1in larger all round than the pan. Roll it up around the rolling pin and unroll over the pie. Press the edges together.

— VARIATIONS —

If covering a pie dish, roll the dough to a round or oval 2in larger than the dish. Cut a 1in strip from the outside and lay this on the moistened rim of the dish. Brush the strip with water and lay the sheet of dough on top. Press edges of the pastry to seal, then trim even with the rim. Knock up the edge with a knife.

Apple Pie

Combine about 2lb peeled, cored and thinly sliced Granny Smith apples, 1 tbsp flour, ½ cup sugar and ¾ tsp apple pie spice. Toss to coat the fruit evenly with the sugar and flour. Use to fill the two-crust pie. Bake in a 375°F oven for about 45 minutes or until the pastry is golden brown and the fruit is tender (test with a skewer through a slit in the top crust). Cool on a rack.

HOT DESSERTS

On chilly days few things are more appealing than a warming dessert and there are recipes here for every occasion. Family favorites include Queen of Puddings, and Apple Brown Betty, but if you're looking for new, enticing ideas, try the quick and tasty Thai Fried Bananas. For special occasions, Amaretto Soufflé is much easier than you might imagine, and Warm Lemon and Syrup Cake, served with poached pears would make a delectable finale to a winter supper party.

Cinnamon and Coconut Rice

INGREDIENTS

Serves 4–6

¼ cup raisins
2 cups water
1 cup short-grain rice
1 cinnamon stick
2 tbsp sugar
2 cups milk
1 cup canned sweetened coconut milk
½ tsp vanilla extract
1 tbsp butter
⅓ cup desiccated coconut
ground cinnamon, for sprinkling

1 Soak the raisins in a small bowl in enough water to cover.

2 Bring the water to a boil in a medium-sized saucepan. Stir in the rice, cinnamon stick and sugar. Return to a boil, then lower the heat, cover, and simmer gently for 15–20 minutes, until the liquid is absorbed.

3 Meanwhile, blend the milk, coconut milk and vanilla extract together in a bowl. Drain the raisins.

4 Remove the cinnamon stick from the pan of rice. Add the raisins and the milk and coconut mixture and stir to mix. Continue cooking, covered and stirring often, for about 20 minutes, until the mixture is just thick. Do not overcook the rice.

5 Preheat the broiler. Transfer the rice to a flameproof serving dish. Dot with the butter and sprinkle with coconut. Broil about 5in from the heat for about 3–5 minutes, until the top is just browned. Sprinkle with cinnamon. Serve warm, or cold, with cream if you like.

Queen of Puddings

This warming winter dessert has a real old-fashioned flavor – it was developed from a seventeenth-century recipe by Queen Victoria's chefs at Buckingham Palace.

INGREDIENTS

Serves 4
1½ cups fresh bread crumbs
4 tbsp sugar, plus 1 tsp
grated rind of 1 lemon
2½ cups milk
4 eggs
3 tbsp raspberry jam, warmed

1 Stir the bread crumbs, 2 tbsp of the sugar and the lemon rind together in a bowl. Bring the milk to a boil in a saucepan, then stir into the bread crumbs.

2 Separate three of the eggs and beat the yolks with the whole egg. Stir into the bread crumb mixture, pour into a buttered baking dish and leave to stand for 30 minutes.

3 Meanwhile, preheat the oven to 325°F. Bake the dessert for 50–60 minutes, until set.

4 Whisk the egg whites in a large, clean bowl until stiff but not dry, then gradually whisk in the remaining 2 tbsp sugar until the mixture is very thick and glossy, taking care not to overwhip.

5 Spread the jam over the dessert, then spoon over the meringue to cover the top completely. Sprinkle the remaining sugar over the meringue, then bake for a further 15 minutes, until the meringue is beginning to turn a light golden color.

COOK'S TIP

The traditional recipe calls for raspberry jam, but you may like to ring the changes by replacing it with another flavored jam, lemon cheese, marmalade or fruit purée.

Candied Fruit Dessert

INGREDIENTS

Serves 4

2½ tbsp raisins, chopped
2 tbsp brandy (optional)
2½ tbsp candied cherries, halved
2½ tbsp candied angelica, chopped
2 trifle sponge cakes, diced
2oz ratafias, crushed
2 eggs
2 egg yolks
2 tbsp sugar
2 cups light cream or milk
few drops of vanilla extract

---— Cook's Tip ———

The dessert can be cooked in an ordinary baking dish, if preferred, and served from the dish.

1. Soak the raisins in the brandy, if using, for several hours.

2. Butter a 3⅔ cup charlotte mold and arrange some of the cherries and angelica in the base.

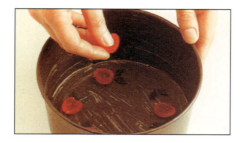

3. Mix the remaining cherries and angelica with the sponge cakes, ratafias and raisins and brandy, if using, and spoon into the mold.

4. Lightly whisk together the eggs, egg yolks and sugar. Bring the cream or milk just to a boil, then stir into the egg mixture with the vanilla extract.

5. Strain the egg mixture into the mold, then leave for 15–30 minutes.

6. Preheat the oven to 325°F. Place the mold in a roasting pan, cover with baking parchment and pour in boiling water. Bake for 1 hour, or until set. Leave for 2–3 minutes, then turn out on to a warm plate.

Eve's Pudding

The tempting apples beneath the sponge topping are the reason for this dessert's name.

INGREDIENTS

Serves 4–6

½ cup butter
½ cup sugar
2 eggs, beaten
grated rind and juice of 1 lemon
scant 1 cup self-rising flour
⅓ cup ground almonds
scant ½ cup brown sugar
1½lb cooking apples, cored and thinly sliced
¼ cup flaked almonds

1. Beat together the butter and sugar in a large mixing bowl using a whisk or wooden spoon until the mixture is very light and fluffy.

2. Gradually beat the eggs into the butter mixture, beating well after each addition, then fold in the lemon rind, flour and ground almonds.

3. Mix the brown sugar, apples and lemon juice, tip into the dish, add the sponge mixture, then the almonds. Bake for 40–45 minutes, until golden.

Apple Brown Betty

INGREDIENTS

Serves 6

1 cup fresh white bread crumbs
¾ cup brown sugar
½ tsp ground cinnamon
¼ tsp ground cloves
¼ tsp grated nutmeg
4 tbsp butter
2lb tart baking apples
juice of 1 lemon
⅓ cup finely chopped walnuts
cream or ice cream, to serve

1 Preheat the broiler. Spread out the bread crumbs on a baking sheet and toast under the broiler until golden brown, stirring frequently to color them evenly. Set aside. Preheat the oven to 375°F. Generously butter a large deep ovenproof dish.

2 Mix the sugar with the cinnamon, cloves and nutmeg. Cut the butter into tiny pieces, then set aside.

3 Peel, core, and slice the apples. Toss immediately with the lemon juice to prevent the apple slices from turning brown.

4 Sprinkle 2–3 tbsp of bread crumbs into the prepared dish. Cover with one-third of the apples and sprinkle with one-third of the sugar and spice mixture. Add another layer of bread crumbs and dot with one-third of the butter. Repeat the layers two more times, ending with a layer of bread crumbs. Sprinkle with the nuts, and dot with the remaining butter.

5 Bake for 35–40 minutes, until the apples are tender and the top is golden brown. Serve warm with cream or ice cream, if you like.

Creole Bread and Butter Pudding

INGREDIENTS

Serves 4–6

4 ready-to-eat dried apricots, chopped
1 tbsp raisins
2 tbsp golden raisins
1 tbsp chopped mixed citrus peel
1 loaf French bread (about 7oz), thinly sliced
4 tbsp butter, melted
1⅞ cups milk
⅔ cup heavy cream
⅝ cup sugar
3 eggs
½ tsp vanilla extract
2 tbsp whiskey

For the cream

⅔ cup heavy cream
2 tbsp thick yogurt
1–2 tbsp whiskey
1 tbsp sugar

1 Preheat the oven to 350°F. Lightly grease a deep 6 cup ovenproof baking dish with butter. Mix together the dried fruits and sprinkle a little over the base of the dish. Brush both sides of the bread slices with melted butter.

2 Fill the dish with alternate layers of bread slices and dried fruit, finishing with a layer of bread.

3 Heat the milk and cream together in a pan until just boiling. Meanwhile, place the sugar, eggs and vanilla extract in a bowl and whisk together.

4 Whisk the hot milk and cream into the eggs and then strain over the bread and fruit. Sprinkle the whiskey over the top. Press the bread into the milk and egg mixture, cover with foil and leave to stand for 20 minutes.

5 Place the dish in a roasting pan half-filled with water and bake for about 1 hour or until the custard is just set. Remove the foil and return the pudding to the oven to cook for a further 10 minutes, until the bread is golden.

6 Just before serving, place the cream, yogurt, whiskey and sugar into a small pan, stir and heat gently. Serve with the hot pudding.

Crêpes Suzette

INGREDIENTS

Makes 8
1 cup flour
pinch of salt
1 egg
1 egg yolk
1¼ cups low-fat (2% or 1%) milk
1 tbsp unsalted butter, melted, plus extra for frying

For the sauce
2 large oranges
4 tbsp butter
½ cup light brown sugar
1 tbsp Grand Marnier
1 tbsp brandy

1 Sift the flour and salt into a bowl and make a well in the center. Crack the egg and extra yolk into the well.

2 Stir the eggs with a wooden spoon to incorporate the flour from around the edges. When the mixture thickens, gradually pour on the milk, beating well after each addition, until a smooth batter is formed.

3 Stir in the butter, transfer to a measuring jug, cover and chill.

4 Heat a medium (about 8in) shallow frying pan, add a little butter and heat until sizzling. Pour on a little of the batter, tilting the pan back and forth to cover the base thinly.

5 Cook over a medium heat for 1–2 minutes until lightly browned underneath, then flip over using a spatula and cook for a further minute. Repeat this process until you have eight crêpes. Stack them up on a plate, as they are ready.

6 Using a zester, pare the rind from one of the oranges and reserve about a teaspoon for decoration. Squeeze the juice from both oranges and set aside.

7 To make the sauce, melt the butter in a large frying pan and add the sugar with the orange rind and juice. Heat gently until the sugar has just dissolved and the mixture is gently bubbling. Fold each crêpe in quarters. Add to the pan one at a time, coating in the sauce and folding each one in half again. Gently move to the side of the pan to make room for the others.

8 Pour on the Grand Marnier and brandy and cook gently for 2–3 minutes, until the sauce has slightly caramelized. (For that extra touch, flame the brandy as you pour it into the pan.) Sprinkle with the reserved orange rind and serve straight from the pan.

Surprise Lemon Dessert

The surprise is a delicious, tangy lemon sauce that forms beneath the light topping.

INGREDIENTS

Serves 4
6 tbsp butter
⅔ cup brown sugar
4 eggs, separated
grated rind and juice of 4 lemons
½ cup self-rising flour
½ cup milk

1 Preheat the oven to 350°F. Butter a 7in soufflé dish or round, deep cake pan and stand the dish or pan in a small roasting pan.

2 Beat the butter and sugar together in a large bowl until pale and very fluffy. Beat in 1 egg yolk at a time, beating well after each addition and gradually beating in the lemon rind and juice until well mixed; do not worry if the mixture curdles a little.

3 Sift the flour and stir into the lemon mixture until well mixed, then gradually stir in the milk.

4 Whisk the egg whites in a separate bowl until stiff but not dry, then lightly, but thoroughly, fold into the lemon mixture in three batches. Carefully pour the mixture into the soufflé dish or cake pan, then pour boiling water around.

5 Bake the dessert in the middle of the oven for about 45 minutes, or until risen, just firm to the touch and golden brown on top. Serve at once.

Spiced Mexican Fritters

Hot, sweet and spicy fritters are popular in both Spain and Mexico either for breakfast or as a mid-morning snack.

INGREDIENTS

Makes 16 (serves 4)
1¼ cups raspberries
3 tbsp confectioner's sugar
3 tbsp orange juice

For the fritters
4 tbsp butter
⅔ cup flour, sifted
2 eggs, lightly beaten
1 tbsp ground almonds
corn oil, for frying
1 tbsp confectioner's sugar and ½ tsp ground cinnamon, for dusting
8 fresh raspberries, to decorate

1 First make the raspberry sauce. Mash the raspberries with the confectioner's sugar and then push through a sieve into a bowl to remove all the seeds. Stir in the orange juice and chill while making the fritters.

2 To make the fritters, place the butter and ⅔ cup water in a saucepan and heat gently until the butter has melted. Bring to a boil and, when boiling, add the sifted flour all at once and turn off the heat.

3 Beat until the mixture leaves the sides of the pan and forms a ball. Cool slightly and beat in the eggs a little at a time, then add the almonds.

4 Spoon the mixture into a piping bag fitted with a large star nozzle. Half-fill a saucepan or deep-fat fryer with the oil and heat to 375°F.

5 Pipe about four 2in lengths at a time into the hot oil, cutting off the raw mixture with a knife as you go. Deep-fry for 3–4 minutes, turning occasionally, until puffed up and golden. Drain on paper towels and keep warm while frying the remainder.

6 When you have fried all the mixture, dust the hot fritters with confectioner's sugar and cinnamon. Serve three or four per person on serving plates drizzled with a little of the raspberry sauce, dust again with sieved sugar and decorate with fresh raspberries.

Thai Fried Bananas

A very simple and quick Thai dessert – bananas fried in butter, brown sugar and lime juice, and then sprinkled with toasted coconut.

INGREDIENTS

Serves 4
3 tbsp butter
4 large slightly underripe bananas
1 tbsp shredded coconut
4 tbsp light brown sugar
4 tbsp lime juice
2 fresh lime slices, to decorate
thick and creamy natural yogurt, to serve

1 Heat the butter in a large frying pan or wok and fry the bananas for 1–2 minutes on each side, or until they are lightly golden in color.

2 Meanwhile, dry-fry the coconut in a small frying pan until lightly browned and reserve.

3 Sprinkle the sugar into the pan with the bananas, add the lime juice and cook, stirring until dissolved. Sprinkle the coconut over the bananas, decorate with lime slices and serve with the thick and creamy yogurt.

Amaretto Soufflé

Ingredients

Serves 6

6 amaretti cookies, coarsely crushed
6 tbsp Amaretto liqueur
4 eggs, separated, plus 1 egg white
7 tbsp sugar
2 tbsp flour
1 cup milk
pinch of cream of tartar (if needed)
a little confectioner's sugar, for dusting

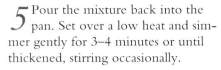

3 Mix together the 4 egg yolks, 2 tbsp of the sugar and flour.

4 Heat the milk just to a boil in a heavy saucepan. Gradually add the hot milk to the egg mixture, stirring.

1 Preheat the oven to 400°F. Butter a 6 cup soufflé dish and sprinkle it with sugar.

2 Put the cookies in a bowl. Sprinkle them with 2 tbsp of the Amaretto liqueur and set aside.

5 Pour the mixture back into the pan. Set over a low heat and simmer gently for 3–4 minutes or until thickened, stirring occasionally.

6 Add the remaining Amaretto liqueur. Remove from the heat.

7 In a scrupulously clean, grease-free bowl, whisk the 5 egg whites until they will hold soft peaks. (If not using a copper bowl, add the cream of tartar as soon as the whites are frothy.) Add the remaining sugar and whisk until stiff.

8 Add about one-quarter of the whites to the liqueur mixture and stir in with a rubber spatula. Add the remaining whites and fold in gently.

9 Spoon half of the mixture into the prepared soufflé dish. Cover with a layer of the moistened amaretti cookies, then spoon the remaining soufflé mixture on top.

10 Bake for 20 minutes or until the soufflé is risen and lightly browned. Sprinkle with sifted confectioner's sugar and serve immediately.

COOK'S TIP

Some people like soufflés to be completely cooked. Others prefer a soft, creamy center. The choice is up to you. To check how cooked the middle is, insert a thin skewer into the center: it will come out almost clean or with some moist particles clinging to it.

Warm Lemon and Syrup Cake

INGREDIENTS

Serves 8
3 eggs
¾ cup butter, softened
¾ cup sugar
1½ cups self-rising flour
½ cup ground almonds
¼ tsp freshly grated nutmeg
2oz candied lemon peel, finely chopped
grated rind of 1 lemon
2 tbsp lemon juice
poached pears, to serve

For the syrup
¾ cup sugar
juice of 3 lemons

1 Preheat the oven to 350°F. Grease and line the base of a deep, round 8in cake pan.

2 Place all the cake ingredients in a large bowl and beat well for 2–3 minutes, until light and fluffy.

3 Tip the mixture into the prepared pan, spread level and bake for 1 hour, or until golden and firm to the touch.

4 Meanwhile, make the syrup. Put the sugar, lemon juice and 5 tbsp water in a pan. Heat gently, stirring until the sugar has dissolved, then boil, without stirring, for 1–2 minutes.

5 Turn out the cake on to a plate with a rim. Prick the surface of the cake all over with a fork, then pour over the hot syrup. Leave to soak for about 30 minutes. Serve the cake warm with thin wedges of poached pears.

Apple Strudel

This Austrian dessert is traditionally made with paper-thin layers of buttered strudel pastry, filled with spiced apples and nuts. Ready-made filo pastry makes an easy substitute.

INGREDIENTS

Serves 4–6

¾ cup chopped hazelnuts, roasted
2 tbsp almonds, roasted
4 tbsp raw sugar
½ tsp ground cinnamon
grated rind and juice of ½ lemon
2 large firm, tart baking apples, peeled, cored and chopped
⅓ cup golden raisins
4 large sheets filo pastry
4 tbsp unsalted butter, melted
confectioner's sugar, for dusting
cream, custard or yogurt, to serve

1 Preheat the oven to 375°F. In a bowl mix together the hazelnuts, almonds, sugar, ground cinnamon, lemon rind and juice, apples and golden raisins, then set aside.

2 Lay one sheet of filo pastry on a clean dish towel and brush with melted butter. Lay a second sheet on top and brush again with melted butter. Repeat with the remaining two sheets.

3 Spread the fruit and nut mixture over the pastry, leaving a 3in border at each of the shorter ends. Fold the pastry ends in over the filling. Roll up from one long edge to the other, using the dish towel to help.

4 Carefully transfer the strudel to a greased baking sheet, placing the seam side down. Brush all over with butter and bake for 30–35 minutes, until golden and crisp. Dust with confectioner's sugar and serve while still hot with cream, custard or yogurt.

Chocolate Fruit Fondue

Fondues originated in Switzerland, and this sweet treat is the perfect ending to any meal.

INGREDIENTS

Serves 6–8

16 fresh strawberries
4 rings fresh pineapple, cut into wedges
2 small nectarines, pitted and cut into wedges
1 kiwi fruit, halved and thickly sliced
small bunch of black seedless grapes
2 bananas, chopped
1 small eating apple, cored and cut into wedges
lemon juice, for brushing
8oz semisweet chocolate
1 tbsp butter
⅔ cup light cream
3 tbsp Irish cream liqueur
1 tbsp pistachio nuts, chopped

1 Arrange the fruit on a serving platter and brush the banana and apple pieces with a little lemon juice. Cover and chill until ready to serve.

2 Place the chocolate, butter, cream and liqueur in a heatproof bowl over a pan of gently simmering water. Stir occasionally until melted and completely smooth.

3 Pour the chocolate mixture into a warmed serving bowl and sprinkle with the pistachios. To serve, guests help themselves by skewering fruits on to fondue forks or dessert forks and dipping in the hot chocolate sauce.

COLD DESSERTS

Chilled desserts are perfect to make when you are entertaining and there are classic dinner party desserts here, such as White Chocolate Parfait, Chocolate Chestnut Roulade, and Peach Melba, as well as some innovative variations on old ideas that are sure to impress. Try the light, tangy cheesecake served in individual slices atop brandy snaps, or the glittering, dark coffee jellies. But that's not all; there are everyday desserts, too, and Apricot Mousse, and Rhubarb and Orange Fool are just as delicious to eat.

Gooseberry Cream

Look out for large "dessert" gooseberries with a slight tawny blush, they are wonderfully sweet – perfect for this cream.

INGREDIENTS

Serves 4
1¼lb gooseberries, topped and tailed
1¼ cups heavy cream
about 1 cup confectioner's
  sugar, to taste
2 tbsp orange flower water
  (optional)
mint sprigs, to decorate
almond cookies, to serve

1 Place the gooseberries in a heavy saucepan, cover and cook over a low heat, shaking the pan occasionally, until the gooseberries are tender. Tip the gooseberries into a bowl, crush them, then leave to cool completely.

2 Beat the cream until soft peaks form, then fold in half the crushed gooseberries. Sweeten with sugar and add the orange flower water, if using. Sweeten the remaining gooseberries with more confectioner's sugar.

3 Layer the cream mixture and the crushed gooseberries in four dessert dishes or tall glasses, then cover and chill. Decorate with mint sprigs and serve with almond cookies.

--- COOK'S TIP ---

If preferred, the cooked gooseberries can be puréed and sieved. An equivalent quantity of real custard can replace the cream.

Honeycomb Mold

These delectable desserts have a fresh, clear lemon flavor. They look attractive when unmolded, as the mixture sets in layers.

INGREDIENTS

Serves 4
2 tbsp cold water
1 tbsp powdered gelatin
2 eggs, separated
scant ½ cup sugar
2 cups milk
grated rind of 1 small lemon
4 tbsp lemon juice

1. Chill four individual molds, or a 5 cup jelly mold.

2. Pour the water into a small bowl, sprinkle over the gelatin and leave to soften for 5 minutes. Place the bowl over a small saucepan of hot water and stir occasionally until dissolved.

3. Meanwhile, whisk the egg yolks and sugar together until pale, thick and fluffy.

4. Bring the milk to a boil in a heavy, preferably nonstick, saucepan, then slowly pour on to the egg yolks, stirring.

5. Return the milk mixture to the pan then heat gently, stirring, until thickened; do not allow to boil. Remove from the heat and stir in the lemon rind and juice.

6. Stir two or three spoonfuls of the lemon mixture into the gelatin, then stir back into the saucepan. In a clean dry bowl, whisk the egg whites until stiff but not dry, then gently fold into the mixture in the saucepan in three batches.

7. Rinse the molds or mold with cold water and drain well, then pour in the lemon mixture. Leave to cool, then cover and chill until set and ready to unmold and serve.

Raspberry-Honey Cream

INGREDIENTS

Serves 4

4 tbsp clear honey
3 tbsp whiskey
⅔ cup medium oatmeal
1¼ cups heavy cream
12oz raspberries
mint sprigs, to decorate

1. Gently warm the honey in the whiskey, then leave to cool.

2. Preheat the broiler. Spread the oatmeal in a very shallow layer in the broiler pan and toast, stirring occasionally, until browned. Leave to cool.

3. Whip the cream in a large bowl until soft peaks form, then gently stir in the oats, honey and whiskey until well combined.

4. Reserve a few raspberries for decoration, then layer the remainder with the oat mixture in four tall glasses. Cover and chill for 2 hours.

5. About 30 minutes before serving, transfer the glasses to room temperature. Decorate with the reserved raspberries and mint sprigs.

Summer Fruit Trifle

INGREDIENTS

Serves 6

3oz day-old sponge cake, broken into bite-size pieces
8 ratafias, broken into halves
⅓ cup medium sherry
2 tbsp brandy
12oz prepared fruit such as raspberries, strawberries or peaches
1¼ cups heavy cream
⅓ cup toasted flaked almonds
strawberries, to decorate

For the custard

4 egg yolks
2 tbsp sugar
scant 2 cups light or whipping cream
few drops of vanilla extract

1. Put the sponge cake and ratafias in a glass serving dish, then sprinkle over the sherry and brandy and leave until they have been absorbed.

2. To make the custard, whisk the egg yolks and sugar together. Bring the cream to a boil in a heavy saucepan, then pour on to the egg yolk mixture, stirring constantly.

3. Return the mixture to the pan and heat very gently, stirring all the time with a wooden spoon, until the custard thickens enough to coat the back of the spoon; do not allow to boil. Leave to cool, stirring occasionally.

4. Put the fruit in an even layer over the sponge cake in the serving dish, then strain the custard over the fruit and leave to set. Lightly whip the cream, spread it over the custard, then chill the trifle well. Decorate with flaked almonds and strawberries just before serving.

Chocolate Mold

For a special dinner party, flavor the custard with peppermint extract, crème de menthe or orange liqueur, and decorate with whipped cream and white and dark chocolate curls.

INGREDIENTS

Serves 4
4 tbsp cornstarch
2½ cups milk
3 tbsp sugar
2–4oz semisweet chocolate, chopped
few drops vanilla extract
chocolate curls, to decorate

1 Rinse a 3 cup fluted mold with cold water and leave it upside-down to drain. Blend the cornstarch to a smooth paste with a little of the milk.

2 Bring the remaining milk to a boil, preferably in a nonstick saucepan, then pour on to the blended mixture stirring all the time.

3 Pour all the milk back into the saucepan and bring slowly to a boil over a low heat, stirring all the time until the mixture boils and thickens. Remove the saucepan from the heat, then add the sugar, chopped chocolate and vanilla extract and stir until the sauce is smooth and the chocolate melted.

4 Pour the chocolate mixture into the mold and leave in a cool place for several hours to set.

5 To unmold the custard, place a large serving plate over the mold, then holding the plate and mold firmly together, invert them. Give both plate and mold a gentle but firm shake to loosen the custard, then lift off the mold. Scatter the white and dark chocolate curls over the top of the custard and serve at once.

COOK'S TIP

If you prefer, set the custard in four or six individual molds.

Australian Hazelnut Pavlova

INGREDIENTS

Serves 4–6

3 egg whites
⅞ cup superfine sugar
1 tsp cornstarch
1 tsp white wine vinegar
5 tbsp chopped hazelnuts, roasted
1 cup heavy cream
1 tbsp orange juice
2 tbsp thick and creamy natural yogurt
2 ripe nectarines, pitted and sliced
2 cups raspberries, halved
1–2 tbsp red currant or raspberry jelly, warmed

1 Preheat the oven to 275°F. Lightly grease a baking sheet. Draw an 8in circle on a sheet of parchment paper. Place pencil-side down on the greased baking sheet.

2 Place the egg whites in a clean, grease-free bowl and whisk with an electric mixer until stiff. Whisk in the sugar 1 tbsp at a time, whisking well after each addition.

3 Add the cornstarch, vinegar and hazelnuts and fold in carefully with a large metal spoon.

4 Spoon the meringue on to the marked circle and spread out to the edges, making a dip in the center.

5 Bake for about 1¼–1½ hours, until crisp. Leave to cool completely and transfer to a serving platter.

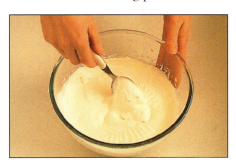

6 Whip the cream and orange juice until just thick, stir in the yogurt and spoon on to the meringue. Top with the fruit and drizzle over the warmed jelly. Serve immediately.

Peach Melba

The original dish created for the opera singer Dame Nellie Melba had peaches and ice cream served upon an ice swan.

INGREDIENTS

Serves 4
11oz raspberries
squeeze of lemon juice
confectioner's sugar, to taste
2 large ripe peaches or 1 x 15oz can sliced peaches
8 scoops vanilla ice cream

1 Press the raspberries through a non-metallic strainer.

2 Add a little lemon juice to the raspberry purée and sweeten to taste with confectioner's sugar.

3 Dip fresh peaches in boiling water for 4–5 seconds, then slip off the skins, halve along the indented line, then slice, or tip canned peaches into a strainer and drain.

4 Place two scoops of ice cream in each individual glass dish, top with peach slices, then pour over the raspberry purée. Serve immediately.

—— COOK'S TIP ——

If you'd like to prepare this ahead, scoop the ice cream on to a cold baking sheet and freeze until ready to serve, then transfer the scoops to the dishes.

Summer Fruit Dessert

INGREDIENTS

Serves 4
about 8 thin slices day-old white bread, crusts removed
1¾lb mixed summer fruits
about 2 tbsp sugar

1 Cut a round from one slice of bread to fit in the base of a 5 cup mixing bowl, then cut strips of bread about 2in wide to line the bowl, overlapping the strips slightly.

2 Gently heat the fruit, sugar and 2 tbsp water in a large heavy saucepan, shaking the pan occasionally, until the juices begin to run.

3 Reserve about 3 tbsp fruit juice, then spoon the fruit and remaining juice into the bowl, taking care not to dislodge the bread.

4 Cut the remaining bread to fit entirely over the fruit. Stand the bowl on a plate and cover with a saucer or small plate that will just fit inside the top of the bowl. Place a heavy weight on top. Chill the dessert and the reserved fruit juice overnight.

5 Run a knife carefully around the inside of the bowl rim, then invert the dessert on to a cold serving plate. Pour over the reserved juice and serve.

Strawberry Cream

This dessert is so easy to put together and yet tastes quite divine – it can be frozen too, for an iced dessert.

INGREDIENTS

Serves 4
1¼lb strawberries, chopped
3–4 tbsp Kirsch
1¼ cups heavy cream
6 small white meringues
mint sprigs, to decorate

1 Put the strawberries in a bowl, sprinkle over the Kirsch, then cover and chill for 2–3 hours.

2 Whip the cream until soft peaks form, then gently fold in the strawberries with their juices.

3 Crush the meringues into rough chunks, then scatter over the strawberry mixture and fold in gently.

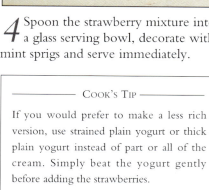

4 Spoon the strawberry mixture into a glass serving bowl, decorate with mint sprigs and serve immediately.

--- COOK'S TIP ---

If you would prefer to make a less rich version, use strained plain yogurt or thick plain yogurt instead of part or all of the cream. Simply beat the yogurt gently before adding the strawberries.

Lemon Cheesecake on Brandy Snaps

Cheating with ready-made brandy snaps gives a quick and crunchy golden base to a simple classic cheesecake mixture.

INGREDIENTS

Serves 8
3oz package lemon Jell-o
2 cups low-fat cream cheese
2 tsp grated lemon rind
about ½ cup sugar
few drops vanilla extract
⅔ cup thick plain yogurt
8 brandy snaps
mint leaves and confectioner's sugar, to decorate

1 Dissolve the Jell-o in ½ cup boiling water in a heatproof measuring jug and, when clear, add sufficient cold water to make up to ⅔ cup. Chill the jelly until beginning to set and thicken slightly. Line a 1lb loaf pan with plastic wrap.

2 Cream the low-fat cream cheese with the lemon rind, sugar and vanilla extract and beat until light and smooth. Then fold in the thickening lemon jelly and the yogurt. Spoon into the prepared pan and chill until set. Preheat the oven to 325°F.

3 Place two or three brandy snaps at a time on a baking sheet. Place in the oven for no more than 1 minute, until soft enough to unroll and flatten out completely. Leave on a cold plate or tray to harden again. Repeat with the remaining brandy snaps.

4 To serve, turn the cheesecake out on to a board with the help of the plastic wrap. Cut into eight slices and place one slice on each brandy snap base. Decorate with mint leaves and sprinkle with confectioner's sugar.

COOK'S TIP

If you don't have any brandy snaps to hand, you could serve this cheesecake on thin slices of moist ginger cake, or on other thin, crisp cookies.

Coffee, Vanilla and Chocolate Stripe

INGREDIENTS

Serves 6

1½ cups sugar
6 tbsp cornstarch
4 cups milk
3 egg yolks
6 tbsp unsalted butter, at room temperature
generous 1 tbsp instant coffee powder
2 tsp vanilla extract
2 tbsp cocoa powder
whipped cream, to serve

3 Divide the coffee mixture among six wine glasses. Smooth the tops before the mixture sets.

7 To make the chocolate layer, place the remaining sugar and cornstarch in a heavy-based saucepan. Gradually whisk in the remaining milk and continue whisking until blended. Over a medium heat, whisk in the last egg yolk and bring to a boil, whisking constantly. Boil for 1 minute. Remove from the heat, stir in the remaining butter and the cocoa. Leave to cool slightly, then spoon into the glasses on top of the vanilla layer. Chill until set.

1 To make the coffee layer, place ½ cup of the sugar and 30ml/2 tbsp of the cornstarch in a heavy-based saucepan. Gradually add one-third of the milk, whisking until well blended. Over a medium heat, whisk in one of the egg yolks and bring to a boil, whisking. Boil for 1 minute.

4 Wipe any dribbles on the insides and outsides of the glasses with damp paper towels.

5 To make the vanilla layer, place half of the remaining sugar and cornstarch in a heavy-based saucepan. Whisk in 1⅓ cups of the milk. Over a medium heat, whisk in another egg yolk and bring to a boil, whisking. Boil for 1 minute.

8 Pipe swirls of whipped cream on top of each dessert before serving.

COOK'S TIP

For a special occasion, prepare the vanilla layer using a fresh vanilla pod. Choose a plump, supple pod and split it down the center with a sharp knife. Add to the mixture with the milk and discard the pod before spooning the mixture into the glasses. The flavor will be more pronounced and the pudding will have pretty brown speckles from the vanilla seeds.

2 Remove the pan from the heat. Stir in 2 tbsp of the butter and the instant coffee powder. Set aside in the pan to cool slightly.

6 Remove the pan from the heat and stir in 2 tbsp of the butter and the vanilla. Leave to cool slightly, then spoon into the glasses on top of the coffee layer. Smooth the tops and wipe the glasses with paper towels.

Orange and Lemon Fool

This fool became the specialty of Boodles Club, a gentlemen's club in London's St James's.

INGREDIENTS

Serves 4

1½ cups cubed spongecake
1¼ cups heavy cream
2–4 tbsp sugar
grated rind and juice of 2 oranges
grated rind and juice of 1 lemon
orange and lemon slices and rind, to decorate

1 Line the bottom and halfway up the sides of a large glass serving bowl or china dish with the cubes of spongecake.

2 Whip the cream with the sugar until it starts to thicken, then gradually whip in the fruit juices, adding the fruit rinds toward the end.

3 Carefully pour the cream mixture into the bowl or dish, taking care not to dislodge the sponge. Cover and chill for 3–4 hours. Serve decorated with orange and lemon slices and rind.

—— WATCHPOINT ——
Take care not to overwhip the cream mixture it should just hold soft peaks.

Apricot and Orange Jelly

INGREDIENTS

Serves 4

12oz well-flavored fresh ripe apricots, pitted
about ⅓ cup sugar
about 1¼ cups freshly squeezed orange juice
1 tbsp powdered gelatin
light cream, to serve
finely chopped candied orange peel, to decorate

1 Heat the apricots, sugar and ½ cup orange juice, stirring until the sugar has dissolved. Simmer gently until the apricots are tender.

2 Press the apricot mixture through a nylon strainer into a small measuring jug.

3 Pour 3 tbsp orange juice into a small heatproof bowl, sprinkle over the gelatin and leave for about 5 minutes, until softened.

4 Place the bowl over a saucepan of hot water and heat until the gelatin has dissolved. Slowly pour into the apricot mixture, stirring all the time. Make up to 2½ cups with orange juice.

5 Pour the apricot mixture into four individual dishes and chill until set. Pour a thin layer of cream over the surface of the jellies before serving, decorated with candied orange peel.

Fruit and Rice Ring

This unusual rice dessert looks beautiful turned out of a ring mold but if you prefer, stir the fruit into the rice and serve in individual dishes.

INGREDIENTS

Serves 4
5 tbsp short-grain rice
3¾ cups skim milk
1 cinnamon stick
1½ cups mixed dried fruit
¾ cup orange juice
3 tbsp sugar
finely grated rind of 1 small orange

1 Place the rice, milk, and cinnamon stick in a large pan and bring to a boil. Cover and simmer, stirring occasionally, for about 1½ hours, until no liquid remains.

2 Meanwhile, place the fruit and orange juice in another pan and bring to a boil. Cover and simmer very gently for about 1 hour, until tender and no liquid remains.

3 Remove the cinnamon stick from the rice and stir in the sugar and orange rind.

4 Tip the fruit into the base of a lightly oiled 6 cup ring mold. Spoon the rice over, smoothing down firmly. Chill until firm.

5 Run a knife around the edge of the mold and turn out the rice carefully on to a serving plate.

Raspberry-Passionfruit Swirls

If passionfruit is not available, this simple dessert can be made with raspberries alone.

INGREDIENTS

Serves 4
2½ cups raspberries
2 passionfruit
1⅔ cups low-fat ricotta cheese
2 tbsp sugar
raspberries and sprigs of mint, to decorate

1 Mash the raspberries in a small bowl with a fork until the juice runs. Scoop out the passionfruit pulp into a separate bowl with the ricotta cheese and sugar and mix well.

2 Spoon alternate spoonfuls of the raspberry pulp and the cheese mixture into stemmed glasses or one large serving dish, stirring lightly to create a swirled effect.

3 Decorate each dessert with a whole raspberry and a sprig of fresh mint. Serve chilled.

COOK'S TIP

Over-ripe, slightly soft fruit can also be used in this recipe. You could use frozen raspberries when fresh are not available, but thaw them first.

VARIATIONS

Other summer fruits would be just as delicious – try a mix of strawberries and red currants with the raspberries, or use mangoes, peaches or apricots which you will need to purée in a food processor or blender before mixing with the ricotta cheese.

Apricots with Orange Cream

Mascarpone is a very rich cream cheese made from thick Lombardy cream. It is delicious flavored with orange as a topping for these poached, chilled apricots.

Ingredients

Serves 4

2½ cups ready-to-eat dried apricots
strip of lemon peel
1 cinnamon stick
3 tbsp sugar
⅔ cup sweet dessert wine (such as Muscat de Beaumes de Venise or Sauternes)
½ cup mascarpone cream cheese or sour cream
3 tbsp orange juice
pinch of ground cinnamon and fresh mint sprig, to decorate

1 Place the dried apricots, lemon peel, cinnamon stick and 2 tbsp of sugar in a pan and cover with 2 cups cold water. Bring to a boil, cover the pan and then simmer gently for about 25 minutes, until the fruit is tender.

2 Remove from the heat and stir in the dessert wine. Leave until cold, then chill for 3–4 hours or overnight.

3 Mix together the mascarpone cheese or sour cream, orange juice and sugar in a bowl and beat well until smooth. Chill until required.

4 Just before serving remove the cinnamon stick and lemon peel from the apricots and serve with a spoonful of the chilled mascarpone orange cream sprinkled with a little cinnamon and decorated with a sprig of fresh mint.

Rhubarb and Orange Fool

Perhaps this traditional English dessert got its name because it is so easy to make that even a "fool" can attempt it.

Ingredients

Serves 4

2 tbsp orange juice
1 tsp finely shredded orange rind
2lb (about 10–12 stems) rhubarb, peeled and chopped
1 tbsp red currant jelly
3 tbsp superfine sugar
5oz prepared thick and creamy vanilla custard
⅔ cup heavy cream, whipped
sweet cookies, to serve

1 Place the orange juice and rind, the rhubarb, red currant jelly and sugar into a saucepan. Cover and simmer gently for about 8 minutes, stirring occasionally, until the rhubarb is just tender but not mushy.

2 Remove the pan from the heat, transfer the rhubarb to a bowl and leave to cool completely. Meanwhile, beat the cream lightly.

3 Drain the cooled rhubarb to remove some of the liquid. Reserve a few pieces of the rhubarb and a little orange rind for decoration. Purée the remaining rhubarb in a food processor or blender, or push through a strainer.

4 Stir the custard into the purée, then fold in the whipped cream. Spoon the fool into individual bowls, cover and chill. Just before serving, top with the reserved fruit and rind. Serve with crisp, sweet cookies.

Apricot Mousse

This light, fluffy dessert can be made with any dried fruits instead of apricots – try dried peaches, prunes, or apples.

INGREDIENTS

Serves 4
1½ cups dried apricots
1¼ cups fresh orange juice
1 cup low-fat ricotta cheese
2 egg whites
mint sprigs, to decorate

1 Place the apricots in a saucepan with the orange juice and heat gently until boiling. Cover the pan and simmer gently for 3 minutes.

2 Cool slightly. Place in a food processor or blender and process until smooth. Stir in the ricotta.

3 Whisk the egg whites until stiff enough to hold soft peaks, then fold into the apricot mixture.

4 Spoon into four stemmed glasses or one large serving dish. Chill before serving, decorated with mint.

COOK'S TIP

For an even quicker version, omit the egg whites and simply swirl together the apricot mixture and ricotta.

WATCHPOINT

This dessert contains raw egg whites and so should not be served to young children, pregnant women or the sick.

Chocolate Fudge Sundaes

INGREDIENTS

Serves 4
4 scoops each vanilla and coffee
   ice cream
2 small ripe bananas, sliced
whipped cream
toasted flaked almonds

For the sauce
¼ cup brown sugar
½ cup corn syrup
3 tbsp strong black coffee
1 tsp ground cinnamon
5oz semisweet chocolate, chopped
⅓ cup whipping cream
3 tbsp coffee liqueur (optional)

1. To make the sauce, place the brown sugar, syrup, coffee and cinnamon in a heavy-based saucepan. Bring to a boil, then boil for about 5 minutes, stirring constantly.

2. Turn off the heat and stir in the chocolate. When melted and smooth, stir in the cream and liqueur, if using. Leave the sauce to cool slightly. If made ahead, reheat the sauce gently until just warm.

3. Fill four glasses with a scoop each of vanilla and coffee ice cream.

4. Scatter the sliced bananas over the ice cream. Pour the warm fudge sauce over the bananas, then top each sundae with a generous swirl of whipped cream. Sprinkle with toasted almonds and serve at once.

VARIATIONS

Vary this recipe by using other flavors of ice cream such as strawberry, toffee or chocolate. In the summer, substitute raspberries or strawberries for the bananas, and scatter chopped roasted hazelnuts on top in place of the flaked almonds.

White Chocolate Parfait

INGREDIENTS

Serves 10
8oz white chocolate, chopped
2½ cups whipping cream
½ cup milk
10 egg yolks
1 tbsp sugar
½ cup desiccated coconut
½ cup canned sweetened coconut milk
5oz unsalted macadamia nuts

For the chocolate icing
8oz semisweet chocolate
6 tbsp butter
1 generous tbsp corn syrup
¾ cup whipping cream
curls of fresh coconut, to decorate

1 Carefully line the bottom and sides of a 6 cup terrine mold (10 x 4in) with plastic wrap.

2 Place the white chocolate and ¼ cup of the cream in the top of a double boiler or in a heatproof bowl set over hot water. Stir until melted and smooth. Set aside.

3 Put 1 cup of the whipping cream and the milk in a pan and bring to boiling point.

4 Meanwhile, whisk the egg yolks and sugar together in a large bowl, until thick and pale.

5 Add the hot cream mixture to the yolks, beating constantly. Pour back into the saucepan and cook over a low heat for 2–3 minutes, until thickened. Stir constantly and do not boil. Remove the pan from the heat.

6 Add the melted chocolate, desiccated coconut and coconut milk, then stir well and leave to cool.

7 Whip the remaining cream until thick, then fold into the chocolate and coconut mixture.

8 Put 2 cups of the parfait mixture in the prepared mold and spread evenly. Cover and freeze for about 2 hours, until just firm. Cover the remaining mixture and chill.

9 Scatter the macadamia nuts evenly over the frozen parfait. Pour in the remaining parfait mixture. Cover the terrine and freeze for 6–8 hours or overnight, until the parfait is firm.

10 To make the icing, melt the chocolate with the butter and syrup in the top of a double boiler set over hot water. Stir occasionally.

11 Heat the cream in a saucepan, until just simmering, then stir into the chocolate mixture. Remove the pan from the heat and leave to cool until lukewarm.

12 To turn out the parfait, wrap the terrine in a hot towel and set it upside-down on a plate. Lift off the terrine mold, then peel off the plastic wrap. Place the parfait on a rack over a baking sheet and pour the chocolate icing evenly over the top. Working quickly, smooth the icing down the sides with a spatula. Leave to set slightly, then freeze for a further 3–4 hours. Cut into slices using a knife dipped in hot water. Serve, decorated with coconut curls.

Banana and Passionfruit Whip

This very easy and quickly prepared dessert is delicious served with crisp cookies.

INGREDIENTS

Serves 4
2 ripe bananas
2 passionfruit
6 tbsp sour cream
⅔ cup heavy cream
2 tsp honey
shortcake or ginger cookies, to serve

1 Peel the bananas, then mash them in a bowl to a smooth purée.

2 Halve the passionfruit and scoop out the pulp. Mix with the bananas and sour cream. Whip the cream with the honey until it forms soft peaks.

3 Carefully fold the cream and honey mixture into the fruit mixture. Spoon into four glass dishes and serve at once with the cookies.

Coffee Jellies with Amaretti Cream

This impressive dessert is very easy to prepare. For the best results, use a high-roasted Arabica bean, preferably from a gourmet coffee shop. Grind the beans until filter-fine, then use to make hot strong coffee.

INGREDIENTS

Serves 4
6 tbsp sugar
2 cups hot strong coffee
2–3 tbsp dark rum or coffee liqueur
4 tsp powdered gelatin

For the coffee amaretti cream
⅔ cup heavy or whipping cream
1 tbsp confectioner's sugar, sifted
2–3 tsp instant coffee granules dissolved in 1 tbsp hot water
6 large amaretti cookies, crushed

1 Put the sugar in a pan with 5 tbsp water and stir over a gentle heat until dissolved. Increase the heat and allow the syrup to boil steadily, without stirring, for 3–4 minutes.

2 Stir the hot coffee and rum or coffee liqueur into the syrup. Sprinkle the gelatin over the top and stir until it is completely dissolved.

3 Pour the jelly mixture into four rinsed-out ⅔ cup molds, allow to cool and then leave in the fridge for several hours until set.

4 To make the amaretti cream, lightly whip the cream with the confectioner's sugar until it holds stiff peaks. Stir in the coffee, then gently fold in all but 2 tbsp of the crushed amaretti cookies.

5 Unmold the jellies on to four individual serving plates and spoon a little of the coffee amaretti cream to one side. Dust over the reserved amaretti crumbs and serve at once.

COOK'S TIP

To ensure that the finished jellies are crystal-clear, filter the coffee grounds through a paper filter.

Chocolate Chestnut Roulade

This moist chocolate sponge has a soft, mousse-like texture as it contains no flour. Don't worry if it cracks as you roll it up – this is typical of a good roulade.

INGREDIENTS

Serves 8
6oz semisweet chocolate
2 tbsp strong black coffee
5 eggs, separated
¾ cup sugar
1 cup heavy cream
8oz unsweetened chestnut
    purée
3–4 tbsp confectioner's sugar, plus
    extra for dusting
light cream, to serve

1 Preheat the oven to 350°F. Line a 13 x 9in jelly roll pan with wax paper and brush lightly with oil.

2 Break up the chocolate into a bowl and set over a pan of barely simmering water. Allow the chocolate to melt very gradually, then stir until smooth. Remove the bowl from the pan and stir in the black coffee. Leave the mixture to cool slightly.

3 Whisk the egg yolks and sugar together in a separate, clean bowl, until thick and light, then gently stir in the cooled chocolate and coffee mixture until well combined.

4 Whisk the egg whites in another bowl until they hold stiff peaks. Stir a spoonful into the chocolate mixture to lighten it, then gently fold in the rest.

5 Pour the mixture into the prepared pan, and gently spread level. Bake for 20 minutes. Remove the roulade from the oven, then cover the cooked roulade with a clean dish towel and leave to cool in the pan for several hours, or preferably overnight.

6 Whip the heavy cream until it forms soft peaks. Mix together the chestnut purée and confectioner's sugar until smooth, then fold into the whipped cream.

7 Lay a piece of wax paper on the work surface and dust with confectioner's sugar. Turn out the roulade on to the paper and carefully peel off the lining paper. Trim the sides.

8 Gently spread the chestnut cream evenly over the roulade to within 1in of the edges.

9 Using the wax paper to help you, carefully roll up the roulade as tightly and evenly as possible.

10 Chill the roulade for about 2 hours, then sprinkle liberally with confectioner's sugar. Cut into thick slices and serve with a little light cream poured over each slice.

— COOK'S TIP —

Make sure that you whisk the egg yolks and sugar for at least 5 minutes to incorporate as much air as possible.

PIES AND TARTS

The combination of crisp pastry with a sweet, tangy or creamy filling makes pies and tarts a popular dessert choice. Many are delicious hot or cold, and they are excellent served up with custard, a spoonful of whipped cream or a scoop or two of ice cream. You'll find plenty of variety to choose from. There are traditional fruit pies filled with apple, walnut and pears, rhubarb, or blueberries; delicious classics such as Spiced Pumpkin Pie; and new twists on homey family favorites like Treacle and Oatmeal Tart.

Yorkshire Curd Tart

Ingredients

Serves 8

½ cup butter, diced
2 cups flour
1 egg yolk

For the filling
large pinch of ground allspice
½ cup light brown sugar
3 eggs, beaten
grated rind and juice of 1 lemon
3 tbsp butter, melted
1lb farmer's cheese
scant ½ cup raisins or golden raisins

1 Toss the butter in the flour, then rub it in until the mixture resembles bread crumbs. Stir the egg yolk into the flour mixture with a little water to bind the dough together.

2 Turn the dough on to a lightly floured surface, knead lightly and briefly, then form into a ball. Roll out the pastry thinly and use to line a 8in fluted loose-bottomed quiche pan. Chill for 15 minutes.

3 Preheat the oven to 375°F. To make the filling, mix the ground allspice with the sugar, then stir in the eggs, lemon rind and juice, butter, farmer's cheese and raisins or golden raisins.

4 Pour the filling into the pie shell, then bake for about 40 minutes until the pastry is cooked and the filling is lightly set and golden brown. Serve still slightly warm, cut into wedges, with cream, if you like.

Cook's Tip

Although it's not traditional, you could easily substitute mixed spice for the ground allspice – the flavor will be slightly different, but just as good in this tart.

Sweet Almond Tart

To make an extra-special dessert, serve this old-fashioned pie with whipped cream or ice cream.

INGREDIENTS
Serves 4
8oz ready-made puff pastry
2 tbsp raspberry or apricot jam
2 eggs
2 egg yolks
generous ½ cup superfine sugar
½ cup butter, melted
⅔ cup ground almonds
few drops of almond extract
confectioner's sugar, for sifting

1 Preheat the oven to 400°F. Roll out the pastry on a lightly floured surface and use it to line a 7in pie plate or loose-based quiche pan. Spread the jam over the bottom of the pie shell.

2 Whisk the eggs, egg yolks and sugar together in a large bowl until thick and pale.

3 Gently stir the butter, ground almonds and almond extract into the mixture.

4 Pour the mixture into the pastry case and bake for 30 minutes, until the filling is just set and browned. Sift confectioner's sugar over the top before eating hot, warm or cold.

— COOK'S TIP —

Since this pastry case isn't baked blind first, place a baking sheet in the oven while it preheats, then place the quiche pan on the hot sheet. This will ensure that the bottom of the pie shell cooks right through.

— VARIATION —

Ground hazelnuts are increasingly available and make an interesting change from almonds in this tart. If you are going to grind shelled hazelnuts yourself, first roast them in the oven for 10–15 minutes to bring out the flavor.

Rhubarb Pie

INGREDIENTS

Serves 6
1½ cups flour
½ tsp salt
2 tsp sugar
6 tbsp cold butter or margarine
¼ cup or more ice water
2 tbsp light cream

For the filling
2lb fresh rhubarb, cut into 1in slices
2 tbsp cornstarch
1 egg
1½ cups sugar
1 tbsp grated orange rind

1 To make the pastry, sift the flour, salt and sugar into a bowl. Using a pastry blender or two knives, cut the butter or margarine into the dry ingredients as quickly as possible until the mixture resembles coarse crumbs.

2 Sprinkle with the ice water and mix until the dough holds together. If the dough is too crumbly, add a little more water, 1 tbsp at a time.

COOK'S TIP

Use milk in place of the light cream to glaze the pie, if you prefer. Or for a crisp crust, brush the pastry with water and sprinkle with sugar instead.

3 Gather the dough into a ball, flatten into a round, place in a plastic bag and chill for 20 minutes.

4 Roll out the pastry between two sheets of wax or parchment paper to ⅛in thickness. Use to line a 9in pie dish or pan. Trim all around, leaving ½in overhang. Fold the overhang under the edge and flute. Chill the pie shell and trimmings for at least 30 minutes.

5 To make the filling, put the rhubarb in a bowl, sprinkle with the cornstarch and toss to coat.

6 Preheat the oven to 425°F. Beat the egg with the sugar in a bowl until thoroughly blended, then mix in the orange rind.

7 Stir the sugar mixture into the rhubarb and mix well, then spoon the fruit into the pastry case.

8 Roll out the pastry trimmings. Stamp out decorative shapes with a cookie cutter or cut shapes with a small knife, using a card template as a guide, if you prefer.

9 Arrange the pastry shapes on top of the pie. Brush the shapes and the edge of the pastry case with cream.

10 Bake the pie for 30 minutes. Reduce the oven temperature to 325°F and continue baking for a further 15–20 minutes, until the pastry is golden brown and the rhubarb is tender. Serve hot with cream.

Spiced Pumpkin Pie

Ingredients

Serves 4–6

1½ cups flour
pinch of salt
6 tbsp unsalted butter
1 tbsp superfine sugar
4 cups peeled fresh pumpkin, seeded and cubed, or 2 cups canned pumpkin, drained
⅝ cup light brown sugar
¼ tsp salt
¼ tsp ground allspice
½ tsp ground cinnamon
½ tsp ground ginger
2 eggs, lightly beaten
½ cup heavy cream
whipped cream, to serve

1 Place the flour in a bowl with the salt and butter and rub in with your fingertips until the mixture resembles bread crumbs (or use a food processor).

2 Stir in the sugar, add about 2–3 tbsp water and then mix to a soft dough. Knead the dough lightly on a floured surface. Flatten out into a round, wrap in a plastic bag and leave to chill for about 1 hour.

3 Preheat the oven to 400°F with a baking sheet inside. If you are using raw pumpkin for the pie, steam it for about 15 minutes, or until quite tender, then leave to cool completely. Purée the steamed or canned pumpkin in a food processor or blender until the consistency is very smooth.

4 Roll out the pastry quite thinly and use to line a 9½in (measured across the top) x 1in deep pie pan. Trim off any excess pastry and reserve for the decoration. Prick the base of the pie shell with a fork.

5 Cut as many leaf shapes as you can from the excess pastry and make vein markings with the back of a knife on each. Brush the edge of the pastry with water and stick the leaves all round the edge. Chill.

6 In a bowl mix together the pumpkin purée, sugar, salt, spices, eggs and cream and pour into the pie shell.

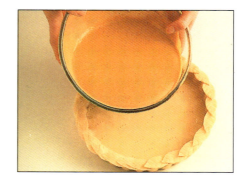

7 Place on the preheated baking sheet and bake for 15 minutes. Then reduce the temperature to 350°F and cook for a further 30 minutes, or until the filling is set and the crust is golden. Serve the pie warm with cream.

Almond Syrup Tart

Ingredients

Serves 6
3oz fresh white bread crumbs
8oz corn syrup
finely grated rind of ½ lemon
2 tsp lemon juice
9in shortcrust pie shell
1oz flaked almonds

1 Preheat the oven to 400°F. In a mixing bowl, combine the bread crumbs with the corn syrup and the lemon rind and juice.

2 Spoon into the pie shell and spread out evenly.

3 Sprinkle the flaked almonds evenly over the top.

4 Brush the pastry with milk to glaze, if you like. Bake for 25–30 minutes or until the pastry and filling are golden brown.

5 Remove to a wire rack to cool. Serve warm or cold, with cream, custard or ice cream.

Variations

For Walnut Syrup Tart, replace the almonds with chopped walnuts. For Ginger Syrup Tart, mix 1 tsp ground ginger with the bread crumbs before adding the syrup and lemon rind and juice. Omit the nuts if liked. For Coconut Syrup Tart, replace 1oz of the bread crumbs with 1½ oz of desiccated coconut.

Peanut Butter Tart

INGREDIENTS

Serves 8

6oz graham crackers, crushed
¼ cup light brown sugar
6 tbsp butter or margarine, melted
whipped cream or ice cream, to serve

For the filling

3 egg yolks
½ cup sugar
¼ cup light brown sugar
¼ cup cornstarch
2½ cups canned evaporated milk
2 tbsp unsalted butter or margarine
1½ tsp vanilla extract
4oz crunchy peanut butter
¾ cup confectioner's sugar

1 Preheat the oven to 350°F. Grease a 9in pie dish.

2 Mix together the cracker crumbs, sugar and butter or margarine in a bowl and blend well. Spread the mixture in the prepared dish, pressing the mixture evenly over the base and sides with your fingertips.

3 Bake the crumb crust for 10 minutes. Remove from the oven and leave to cool. Leave the oven on.

4 To make the filling, mix together the egg yolks, sugars and cornstarch in a heavy-based saucepan using a wooden spoon.

5 Slowly whisk in the milk, then cook over a medium heat for about 8–10 minutes, stirring constantly, until the mixture thickens. Reduce the heat to very low and cook for a further 3–4 minutes, until the mixture is very thick.

6 Beat in the butter or margarine and the vanilla extract. Remove the pan from the heat, then cover the surface loosely with plastic wrap and cool.

─── COOK'S TIP ───
If preferred, use equal amount of finely crushed ginger snaps in place of graham crackers for the crumb crust. Or make the pie with a ready-made pie shell.

7 Combine the peanut butter with the confectioner's sugar in a small bowl, working with your fingertips to blend the ingredients to the consistency of fine bread crumbs.

8 Sprinkle all but 3 tbsp of the peanut butter crumbs evenly over the base of the crumb crust.

9 Pour in the filling, spreading it into an even layer, then top with the remaining crumbs and bake for 15 minutes. Leave the pie to cool for at least 1 hour. Serve with whipped cream or ice cream.

Mississippi Pecan Pie

INGREDIENTS

Makes an 8in pie
For the pastry
1 cup flour
4 tbsp butter, cubed
2 tbsp sugar
1 egg yolk

For the filling
5 tbsp corn syrup
⅓ cup dark brown sugar, firmly packed
4 tbsp butter
3 eggs, lightly beaten
½ tsp vanilla extract
1¼ cups pecan nuts
fresh cream or ice cream, to serve

1 Place the flour in a bowl and add the butter. Rub in the butter with your fingertips until the mixture resembles crumbs, then stir in the sugar, egg yolk and about 2 tbsp cold water. Mix to a dough and knead lightly on a floured surface until smooth.

2 Roll out the pastry on a floured surface and use to line an 8in loose-based fluted pie pan. Prick the base, then line with waxed paper and fill with baking beans. Chill for 30 minutes. Preheat the oven to 400°F.

3 Bake the pie shell for 10 minutes. Remove the paper and beans and bake for 5 minutes. Reduce the oven temperature to 350°F.

4 Meanwhile, heat the syrup, sugar and butter in a pan until the sugar dissolves. Remove from the heat and cool slightly. Whisk in the eggs and vanilla extract and stir in the pecans.

5 Pour into the pie shell and bake for 35–40 minutes, until the filling is set. Serve with cream or ice cream.

Walnut and Pear Lattice Pie

INGREDIENTS

Serves 6–8

12oz shortcrust pastry
2lb pears, peeled, cored and thinly sliced
2oz granulated sugar
1oz flour
½ tsp grated lemon rind
1oz raisins
1oz walnuts, chopped
½ tsp ground cinnamon
2oz confectioner's sugar
1 tbsp lemon juice
about 2 tsp cold water

1 Preheat the oven to 375°F. Roll out half of the pastry dough and use to line a 9in pan that is about 2in deep.

2 Combine the pears, granulated sugar, flour and lemon rind in a bowl. Toss gently until the fruit is evenly coated with the dry ingredients. Mix in the raisins, nuts and cinnamon.

COOK'S TIP

For a simple cutout lattice top, roll out the dough for the top into a circle. Using a small pastry cutter, cut out shapes in a pattern, spacing them evenly and not too close together.

3 Put the pear filling into the pastry case and spread it evenly.

4 Roll out the remaining pastry dough on a floured surface and use to make a lattice top.

5 Bake the pie for 55 minutes or until the pastry is golden brown.

6 Combine the confectioner's sugar, lemon juice and water in a bowl and stir until smoothly blended.

7 Remove the pie from the oven. Drizzle the sugar glaze evenly over the top of the pie, on pastry and filling. Leave the pie to cool, set on a wire rack, before serving.

Oranges with Spiced Cream

INGREDIENTS

Serves 4

3 large oranges
1–2 tbsp raw sugar
⅔ cup thick or sour cream, crème fraîche or strained plain yogurt
1 tsp mixed spice
few drops vanilla extract
sugar, to taste

1 Cut away all the orange rind and white pith using a sharp knife, saving any of the juices. Cut the oranges into thick slices and arrange these on foil in a broiler pan.

2 Sprinkle the orange slices with the sugar. Whisk the cream, crème fraîche or yogurt until smooth, then blend in the mixed spice and vanilla extract and any orange juice. Chill.

3 Place the orange slices under a very hot broiler and broil until browned and bubbling. Transfer the orange slices to serving plates and serve at once with the chilled spiced cream.

Treacle and Oatmeal Tart

Oatmeal always evokes childhood memories. This tart, with its rich molasses flavor, is a far cry from the dutiful hot cereal served on cold winter mornings.

INGREDIENTS

Serves 6–8

1 cup flour
⅔ cup rolled oats
pinch of salt
½ cup butter or margarine
6 tbsp corn syrup
2 tbsp black molasses
grated rind and juice of 1 orange
1½ cups soft white bread or cake crumbs

1 Place the flour, oats, salt and fat in a food processor or blender and process on high for ½–1 minute, until well blended.

2 Turn into a bowl and stir in sufficient water (4–5 tbsp) to bring the pastry together. Knead lightly until smooth, wrap in plastic wrap and chill for 10–20 minutes.

3 Place the syrup, molasses, orange rind and juice in a small pan and warm through gently. Then stir in the crumbs. Preheat the oven to 375°F.

4 Roll out the pastry on a floured surface to a 9in round and use to line a shallow 8in pie plate. Trim the edges neatly, then re-roll the trimmings, cut out leaves and use to decorate the edges.

5 Spread the filling in the pie shell and bake for 25–30 minutes, or until the pastry is crisp.

Pear and Blueberry Pie

Ingredients

Serves 4

2 cups flour
pinch of salt
4 tbsp shortening, cubed
4 tbsp butter, cubed
1½lb blueberries
2 tbsp sugar
1 tbsp arrowroot
2 ripe, but firm pears, peeled, cored and sliced
½ tsp ground cinnamon
grated rind of ½ lemon
beaten egg, to glaze
sugar, for sprinkling
crème fraîche or heavy cream, to serve

1 Sift the flour and salt into a bowl and rub in the shortening and butter until the mixture resembles fine bread crumbs. Stir in 3 tbsp cold water and mix to a dough. Chill for 30 minutes.

2 Place 8oz of the blueberries in a pan with the sugar. Cover and cook gently until the blueberries have softened. Press through a nylon strainer.

3 Blend the arrowroot with 2 tbsp cold water and add to the blueberry purée. Bring to a boil, stirring until thickened. Cool slightly.

4 Place a baking sheet in the oven and preheat to 375°F. Roll out just over half the pastry on a lightly floured surface and use to line an 8in shallow pie pan.

5 Mix together the remaining blueberries, the pears, cinnamon and lemon rind and spoon into the dish. Pour over the blueberry purée.

6 Roll out the remaining pastry and use to cover the pie. Make a small slit in the center. Brush with beaten egg and sprinkle with sugar. Bake the pie on the hot baking sheet, for 40–45 minutes, until golden. Serve warm with crème fraîche or heavy cream.

Blueberry Pie

INGREDIENTS

Serves 6–8

12oz shortcrust pastry
1¼lb blueberries
5½oz sugar
3 tbsp flour
1 tsp grated orange rind
¼ tsp grated nutmeg
2 tbsp orange juice
1 tsp lemon juice

1. Preheat the oven to 375°F. Roll out half of the pastry and use to line a 9in pie pan that is about 2in deep.

2. Combine the blueberries, 5oz of the sugar, the flour, orange rind and nutmeg in a bowl. Toss the mixture gently to coat the fruit evenly with the dry ingredients.

3. Pour the blueberry mixture into the pie shell and spread it evenly. Sprinkle over the citrus juices.

4. Roll out the remaining pastry and cover the pie. Cut out small decorative shapes or cut two or three slits for steam vents. Finish the edge.

5. Brush the top of the pie lightly with water and sprinkle evenly with the remaining sugar.

6. Bake for about 45 minutes or until the pastry is golden brown. Serve warm or at room temperature.

Apple Pie

INGREDIENTS

Serves 8

6 cups peeled and sliced tart apples, such as Granny Smith (about 2lb)
1 tbsp fresh lemon juice
1 tsp vanilla extract
½ cup sugar
½ tsp ground cinnamon
1½ tbsp butter or margarine
1 egg yolk
2 tsp whipping cream

For the crust

2 cups flour
1 tsp salt
¾ cup shortening
4–5 tbsp ice water
1 tbsp quick-cooking tapioca

1. Preheat the oven to 450°F. For the crust, sift the flour and salt into a mixing bowl. Using a pastry blender, cut in the shortening until the mixture resembles coarse crumbs.

2. Sprinkle in the water, 1 tbsp at a time, tossing lightly with your fingertips or with a fork until the dough will form a ball.

3. Divide the dough in half and shape each half into a ball and flatten slightly. On a lightly floured surface, roll out one of the balls to a 12in round.

4. Use it to line a 9in pie pan, easing the dough in and being careful not to stretch it. Trim off the excess dough and use the trimmings for decorating. Sprinkle the tapioca over the base of the bottom of the pie shell.

5. Roll out the remaining dough to ⅛in thickness. With a sharp knife, cut out eight large leaf shapes. Cut the trimmings into small leaf shapes. Score the leaves with the back of the knife to mark veins.

6. In a bowl, toss the apples with the lemon juice, vanilla, sugar and cinnamon. Fill the pie shell with the apple mixture and dot with the butter or margarine.

7. Arrange the large pastry leaves in a decorative pattern on top, then decorate the edge with small leaves.

8. Mix together the egg yolk and cream and brush over the leaves to glaze them.

9. Bake for 10 minutes, then reduce the heat to 350°F, and continue baking until the pastry is golden brown, 35–45 minutes. Let the pie cool in the pan, set on a wire rack.

Mississippi Mud Pie

INGREDIENTS

Serves 8

3oz semisweet chocolate
4 tbsp butter or margarine
3 tbsp corn syrup
3 eggs, beaten
⅔ cup sugar
1 tsp vanilla extract
4oz chocolate bar
2 cups whipping cream

For the crust

1⅓ cups flour
½ tsp salt
½ cup shortening
2–3 tbsp ice water

1. Preheat the oven to 425°F. For the crust, sift the flour and salt into a mixing bowl. Using a pastry blender, cut in the shortening until the mixture resembles coarse crumbs. Sprinkle in the water, 1 tbsp at a time. Toss lightly with your fingers or a fork until the dough will form a ball.

2. On a lightly floured surface, roll out the dough. Use to line an 8 or 9in pie pan, easing in the dough and being careful not to stretch it. With your thumbs, make a fluted edge.

3. Using a fork, prick the bottom and sides of the pie shell all over. Bake until lightly browned, 10–15 minutes. Let the pie shell cool, in the pan, on a wire rack.

4. In a heatproof bowl set over a pan of simmering water, or in a double boiler, melt the 3oz of chocolate, the butter or margarine, and corn syrup. Remove the bowl from the heat and stir in the eggs, sugar and vanilla.

5. Reduce the oven temperature to 350°F. Pour the chocolate mixture into the baked crust. Bake until the filling is set, 35–40 minutes. Let cool completely in the pan, set on a rack.

6. For the decoration, use the heat of your hands to slightly soften the chocolate bar. Draw the blade of a swivel-headed vegetable peeler along the side of the chocolate bar to shave off short, wide curls. Chill the chocolate curls until needed.

7. Before serving, lightly whip the cream until soft peaks form. Using a rubber spatula, spread the cream over the surface of the chocolate filling. Decorate with the chocolate curls.

Banana Cream Pie

INGREDIENTS

Serves 6

2 cups finely crushed ginger snaps
5 tbsp butter or margarine, melted
½ tsp grated nutmeg or ground cinnamon
¾ cup mashed ripe bananas
1½ x 8oz packages cream cheese, at room temperature
¼ cup thick plain yogurt or sour cream
3 tbsp dark rum or 1 tsp vanilla extract

For the topping
1 cup whipping cream
3–4 bananas

1 Preheat the oven to 375°F. In a mixing bowl, combine the cookie crumbs, butter or margarine and spice. Mix thoroughly with a wooden spoon.

2 Press the cookie mixture into a 9in pie pan, building up thick sides with a neat edge. Bake 5 minutes. Let cool, in the pan, on a wire rack.

3 With an electric mixer, beat the mashed bananas with the cream cheese. Fold in the yogurt or sour cream and rum or vanilla. Spread the filling in the crumb crust. Chill at least 4 hours or overnight.

4 For the topping, whip the cream until soft peaks form. Spread on the pie filling. Slice the bananas and arrange on top in a decorative pattern.

FRUIT DESSERTS

Light, tangy and refreshing, simple fruit desserts are particularly appealing after a rich or filling main course. You'll find some enticing treats to try, such as Hot Spiced Bananas, Baked Peaches with Raspberry Sauce, and Tropical Fruits in Cinnamon Syrup, as well as old favorites such as baked apple, poached pears, and a selection of hot fruit compôtes. And, if the meal is a little lighter, Blueberry Pancakes, Fruity Ricotta Creams, or a rich Raspberry Trifle will go down well with just about everyone.

Baked Apples with Apricots

Ingredients

Serves 6

½ cup chopped, ready-to-eat dried apricots
½ cup chopped walnuts
1 tsp grated lemon rind
½ tsp ground cinnamon
½ cup light brown sugar
2 tbsp butter, at room temperature
6 large eating apples
1 tbsp melted butter

1 Place the dried apricots, walnuts, lemon rind and cinnamon in a bowl. Add the sugar and butter and stir until thoroughly mixed.

2 Preheat the oven to 375°F. Core the apples, without cutting all the way through to the base. Peel the top of each apple using a vegetable peeler and slightly widen the top of each opening to make room for the filling.

3 Spoon the filling into the apples, packing it down lightly.

4 Place the stuffed apples in an ovenproof dish large enough to hold them comfortably side by side.

5 Brush the apples with the melted butter. Bake for 40–45 minutes, until they are tender. Serve hot.

Spiced Pears in Cider

Any variety of pear can be used for cooking, but it is best to choose firm pears for this recipe, or they will break up easily – Bosc are a good choice.

INGREDIENTS

Serves 4
4 medium firm pears
1 cup dry cider
thinly pared strip of lemon rind
1 cinnamon stick
2 tbsp brown sugar
1 tsp arrowroot
ground cinnamon, to sprinkle
low-fat yogurt, to serve

1 Peel the pears thinly, leaving them whole with the stems on. Place in a pan with the cider, lemon rind, and cinnamon. Cover and simmer gently, turning the pears occasionally for 15–20 minutes, or until tender.

2 Lift out the pears. Boil the syrup, uncovered, to reduce by about half. Remove the lemon rind and cinnamon stick, then stir in the sugar.

3 Mix the arrowroot with 1 tbsp cold water in a small bowl until smooth, then stir into the syrup. Bring to a boil and stir over the heat until thickened and clear.

4 Pour the sauce over the pears and sprinkle with ground cinnamon. Leave to cool slightly, then serve warm with low-fat yogurt.

COOK'S TIP
Whole pears look very impressive, but if you prefer, they can be halved and cored before cooking. This will reduce the cooking time slightly.

VARIATIONS
Other fruits can be poached in this spicy liquid; try apples, peaches or nectarines. Cook the fruit whole or cut in half or quarters. The apples are best peeled before poaching, but you can cook the peaches and nectarines with their skins on.

Greek Fig and Honey Dessert

A quick and easy dessert made from fresh or canned figs topped with thick and creamy yogurt, drizzled with honey and sprinkled with pistachio nuts.

INGREDIENTS

Serves 4

4 fresh or canned figs
2 x 8oz tubs/2 cups thick and creamy natural yogurt
4 tbsp honey
2 tbsp chopped pistachio nuts

1 Chop the figs and place in the bottom of four stemmed glasses or deep, individual dessert bowls.

2 Top each glass or bowl of figs with ½ cup of the thick yogurt. Chill until ready to serve.

3 Just before serving drizzle 1 tbsp honey over each dessert and sprinkle with the pistachio nuts.

COOK'S TIP

Look out for exotic honeys made from the nectar of flowers like lavender, clover, acacia, heather, rosemary and thyme.

Russian Fruit Compôte

This fruit pudding is traditionally called *Kissel* and is made from the thickened juice of stewed red or black currants. This recipe uses the whole fruit with added blackberry liqueur.

INGREDIENTS

Serves 4

2 cups red or black currants, or a mixture of both
2 cups raspberries
⅔ cup water
4 tbsp sugar
1½ tbsp arrowroot
1–2 tbsp blackberry liqueur
natural yogurt, to serve

1 Place the red or black currants and raspberries, water and sugar in a pan. Cover the pan and cook gently over a low heat for 12–15 minutes, until the fruit is soft.

2 Blend the arrowroot with a little water in a small bowl and stir into the hot fruit mixture. Bring the fruit mixture back to a boil, stirring all the time, until thickened and smooth.

3 Remove the pan from the heat and leave the fruit compôte to cool slightly, and then gently stir in the blackberry liqueur.

4 Pour the compôte into four glass serving bowls and leave until cold, then chill until required. Serve topped with spoonfuls of yogurt.

COOK'S TIP

Instead of blackberry liqueur you could use Crème de Cassis, raspberry liqueur, plum brandy or Kirsch, if you prefer.

Blueberry Pancakes

These are rather like thick breakfast pancakes – though they can, of course, be eaten at any time of the day.

INGREDIENTS

Makes 6–8
1 cup self-rising flour
pinch of salt
3–4 tbsp sugar
2 eggs
½ cup milk
1–2 tbsp oil
4oz fresh or frozen blueberries
maple syrup, to serve

1 Sift the flour into a bowl with the salt and sugar. Beat together the eggs thoroughly. Make a well in the middle of the flour and stir in the eggs.

2 Gradually blend in a little of the milk to make a smooth batter. Then whisk in the rest of the milk and whisk for 1–2 minutes. Allow to rest for 20–30 minutes.

3 Heat a few drops of oil in a pancake pan or heavy-based frying pan until just hazy. Pour on about 2 tbsp of the batter and swirl the batter around until it makes an even shape.

4 Cook for 2–3 minutes and when almost set on top, sprinkle over 1–2 tbsp blueberries. As soon as the base is loose and golden brown, turn the pancake over.

5 Cook on the second side for only about 1 minute, until golden and crisp. Slide the pancake on to a plate and serve drizzled with maple syrup. Continue with the rest of the batter.

COOK'S TIP
Instead of blueberries you could use fresh or frozen blackberries or raspberries. If you use canned fruit, make sure it is very well drained or the liquid will run and color the pancakes.

Apple Soufflé Omelette

Apples sautéed until they are slightly caramelized make a delicious autumn filling – you could use fresh raspberries or strawberries in the summer.

INGREDIENTS

Serves 2
4 eggs, separated
2 tbsp light cream
1 tbsp sugar
1 tbsp butter
confectioner's sugar, for dredging

For the filling
1 apple, peeled, cored and sliced
2 tbsp butter
2 tbsp light brown sugar
3 tbsp light cream

1 To make the filling, sauté the apple slices in the butter and sugar until just tender. Stir in the cream and keep warm, while making the omelette.

2 Place the egg yolks in a bowl with the cream and sugar and beat well. Whisk the egg whites until stiff, then fold into the yolk mixture.

3 Melt the butter in a large heavy-based frying pan, pour in the soufflé mixture and spread evenly. Cook for 1 minute until golden underneath, then place under a hot broiler to brown the top.

4 Slide the omelette on to a plate, add the apple mixture, then fold over. Sift the confectioner's sugar over thickly, then mark in a criss-cross pattern with a hot metal skewer. Serve immediately.

Ruby Plum Mousse

Ingredients

Serves 6
1lb ripe red plums
3 tbsp granulated sugar
4 tbsp ruby port
1 tbsp powdered gelatin
3 eggs, separated
½ cup superfine sugar
⅔ cup heavy cream
skinned and chopped pistachio nuts, to decorate
cinnamon cookies, to serve (optional)

1 Put 3 tbsp water in a small bowl, sprinkle over the gelatin and leave to soften. Stand the bowl in a pan of hot water and leave until dissolved. Stir into the plum purée.

2 Put 3 tbsp water in a small bowl, sprinkle over the gelatin and leave to soften. Stand the bowl in a pan of hot water and leave until dissolved. Stir into the plum purée.

3 Place the egg yolks and superfine sugar in a bowl and whisk until thick and mousse-like. Fold in the plum purée, then whip the cream and fold in gently.

4 Whisk the egg whites until they hold stiff peaks, then carefully fold in using a metal spoon. Divide among six glasses and chill until set.

5 Decorate the mousses with chopped pistachio nuts and serve with crisp cinnamon cookies, if liked.

——— Cook's Tip ———
To make a non-alcoholic mousse, use red grape juice in place of the port.

Warm Autumn Compôte

A simple yet quite sophisticated dessert using autumnal fruits.

Ingredients

Serves 4
6 tbsp sugar
1 bottle red wine
1 vanilla pod, split
1 strip pared lemon rind
4 pears
2 purple figs, quartered
8oz raspberries
lemon juice, to taste

1 Put the sugar and wine in a large pan and heat gently until the sugar is dissolved. Add the vanilla pod and lemon rind and bring to a boil. Simmer for 5 minutes.

2 Peel and halve the pears, then scoop out the cores, using a melon baller. Add the pears to the syrup and poach for 15 minutes, turning the pears several times so they color evenly.

3 Add the figs and poach for a further 5 minutes, until the fruits are tender.

4 Transfer the poached pears and figs to a serving bowl using a slotted spoon, then scatter over the raspberries.

5 Return the syrup to the heat and boil rapidly to reduce slightly and concentrate the flavor. Add a little lemon juice to taste. Strain the syrup over the fruits and serve warm.

Hot Spiced Bananas

Ingredients

Serves 6

6 ripe bananas
1 cup light brown sugar, firmly packed
1 cup unsweetened pineapple juice
½ cup dark rum
2 cinnamon sticks
12 whole cloves

1 Preheat the oven to 350°F. Grease a 9in shallow baking dish or an ovenproof pie plate.

2 Peel the bananas and cut them into 1in pieces on the diagonal. Arrange the banana pieces evenly over the base of the prepared baking dish or pie plate.

3 In a saucepan, combine the sugar and pineapple juice. Cook over medium heat until the sugar has dissolved, stirring occasionally.

4 Add the rum, cinnamon sticks, and cloves. Bring to a boil, and then remove the saucepan from the heat.

5 Pour the pineapple-spice mixture over the bananas. Bake until the bananas are very tender and hot, 25–30 minutes. Serve hot.

Baked Peaches with Raspberry Sauce

INGREDIENTS

Serves 6

3 tbsp unsalted butter, at room temperature
¼ cup sugar
1 egg, beaten
½ cup ground almonds
6 ripe peaches

For the sauce
1 cup raspberries
1 tbsp confectioner's sugar
1 tbsp raspberry liqueur
raspberries and bay leaves, to decorate

1 Beat the butter with the sugar until light and fluffy, then beat in the egg. Add the ground almonds and beat just enough to blend together well.

2 Preheat the oven to 350°F. Halve the peaches with a knife and remove the pits. With a spoon, scrape out a little of the flesh from each peach half, slightly enlarging the hollow left by the pit. Reserve the excess peach flesh for the sauce.

3 Place the peach halves on a baking sheet (if necessary, secure with crumpled foil to keep them steady) and fill the hollow in each peach half with the almond mixture.

4 Bake for about 30 minutes, until the almond filling is puffed and golden and the peaches are very tender.

5 Meanwhile, to make the sauce, place the raspberries, icing sugar and liqueur in a food processor or blender. Add the reserved peach flesh and process until smooth. Press through a strainer to remove the seeds.

6 Leave the peaches to cool slightly, then serve with the raspberry sauce. Decorate each serving with a few raspberries and bay leaves.

Cherries Jubilee

Fresh cherries are wonderful cooked lightly to serve hot over ice cream. Children especially will love this dessert.

INGREDIENTS

Serves 4
1lb red or black cherries
½ cup sugar
pared rind of 1 lemon
1 tbsp arrowroot
4 tbsp Kirsch
vanilla ice cream, to serve

COOK'S TIP

If you don't have a cherry pitter, simply push the stones through with a skewer. Remember to save the juice to use in the recipe.

---

1 Pit the cherries over a pan to catch the juice. Drop the pits into the pan as you work.

2 Add the sugar, lemon rind and 1¼ cups water to the pan. Stir over a low heat until the sugar dissolves, then bring to a boil and simmer for 10 minutes. Strain the syrup, then return to the pan. Add the cherries and cook for 3–4 minutes.

3 Blend the arrowroot to a paste with 1 tbsp cold water and stir into the cherries, off the heat.

4 Return the pan to the heat and bring to a boil, stirring all the time. Cook the sauce for a minute or two, stirring until it is thick and smooth. Heat the Kirsch in a ladle over a flame, ignite and pour over the cherries. Spoon the hot sauce over scoops of ice cream and serve at once.

Apricots in Marsala

Make sure the apricots are completely covered by the syrup so that they don't discolor.

INGREDIENTS

Serves 4
12 apricots
4 tbsp sugar
1¼ cups Marsala
2 strips pared orange rind
1 vanilla pod, split
⅔ cup heavy or whipping cream
1 tbsp confectioner's sugar
¼ tsp ground cinnamon
⅔ cup strained plain yogurt

1 Halve and pit the apricots, then place in a bowl of boiling water for about 30 seconds. Drain well, then carefully slip off their skins.

2 Place the sugar, Marsala, orange rind, vanilla pod and 1 cup water in a pan. Heat gently until the sugar dissolves. Bring to a boil, without stirring, then simmer for 2–3 minutes.

3 Add the apricot halves to the pan and poach them for about 5–6 minutes, or until they are just tender. Using a slotted spoon, transfer the apricots to a serving dish.

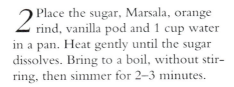

4 Boil the syrup rapidly until it is reduced by half, then pour over the apricots and leave to cool. Cover and chill for several hours. Remove the orange rind and vanilla pod.

5 Whip the cream with the confectioner's sugar and cinnamon until it forms soft peaks. Gently fold in the yogurt. Spoon into a serving bowl and chill until required. Serve with the apricots.

Plum and Port Sorbet

This is more of a sorbet for grown-ups, but you could use red grape juice in place of the port if you prefer.

INGREDIENTS

Serves 4–6
2lb ripe red plums, halved and pitted
6 tbsp sugar
3 tbsp water
3 tbsp ruby port or red wine
plain cookies, to serve

1 Place the plums in a pan with the sugar and water. Stir over gentle heat until the sugar is melted, then cover and simmer gently for about 5 minutes, until the fruit is soft.

2 Turn into a food processor and purée until smooth, then stir in the port. Cool completely, then tip into a freezer container and freeze until firm around the edges.

3 Spoon into the food processor and process until smooth. Return to the freezer and freeze until solid.

4 Allow to soften slightly at room temperature for 15–20 minutes before serving in scoops, with plain cookies.

COOK'S TIP

You could use other fruits in place of the plums; try peaches or pears for a change.

Mango Sorbet

Ingredients

Serves 6

¾ cup sugar
¾ cup water
a large strip of orange rind
1 large mango, peeled, pitted, and cubed
4 tbsp orange juice

1 Combine the sugar, water and orange rind in a saucepan. Bring to a boil, stirring to dissolve the sugar. Leave the sugar syrup to cool.

2 Purée the mango with the orange juice in a blender or food processor. There should be about 2 cups of purée.

3 Add the mango purée to the cooled sugar syrup and mix well, then strain. Taste the mixture (it should be well flavored). Chill.

4 When cold, tip the mango mixture into a freezer container and freeze until firm around the edges.

5 Spoon the semi-frozen mixture into the food processor and process until smooth. Return to the freezer and freeze until solid. Allow the sorbet to soften slightly at room temperature for 15–20 minutes before serving in scoops.

COOK'S TIP

To freeze the sorbet very quickly use a wide, shallow container and place it directly on the freezer shelf. Turn the freezer to its lowest setting about 1 hour before making the sorbet so that it has time to get really cold.

VARIATIONS

- For Banana Sorbet: peel and cube 4–5 large bananas. Purée with 2 tbsp lemon juice to make 2 cups. If liked, replace the orange rind in the sugar syrup with 2–3 whole cloves, or omit the rind.
- For Papaya Sorbet: peel, seed and cube 1½lb papaya. Purée with 3 tbsp lime juice to make 2 cups. Replace the orange rind with lime rind.
- For Passionfruit Sorbet: halve 16 or more passionfruit and scoop out the seeds and pulp (there should be about 2 cups). Work in a blender or food processor until the seeds are like coarse pepper. Omit the orange juice and rind. Add the passionfruit to the sugar syrup, then press through a wire strainer before freezing.

Fruit Kabobs with Mango-Yogurt Sauce

INGREDIENTS

Serves 4

½ cup pineapple, peeled, cored, and cubed
2 kiwis, peeled and cubed
½ pint strawberries, hulled and cut in half lengthwise, if large
½ mango, peeled, pitted, and cubed

For the sauce

½ cup fresh mango purée, from 1–1½ peeled and pitted mangoes
½ cup thick plain yogurt
1 tsp sugar
⅛ tsp vanilla extract
1 tbsp finely shredded fresh mint leaves

1 To make the sauce, beat together the mango purée, yogurt, sugar, and vanilla with an electric mixer.

2 Stir in the chopped mint. Cover the sauce and chill until required.

3 Thread the fruit on to twelve 6in wooden skewers, alternating the pineapple, kiwis, strawberries, and mango cubes.

4 Arrange the kabobs on a large serving tray with the mango-yogurt sauce in the center.

Tropical Fruits in Cinnamon Syrup

INGREDIENTS

Serves 6

2 cups sugar
1 cinnamon stick
1 large or 2 medium papayas (about 1½lb), peeled, seeded, and cut lengthwise into thin pieces
1 large or 2 medium mangoes (about 1½lb), peeled, pitted, and cut lengthwise into thin pieces
1 large or 2 small starfruit (about ½lb), thinly sliced

1 Sprinkle ⅔ cup of the sugar over the bottom of a large saucepan. Add the cinnamon stick and half the papaya, mango, and starfruit pieces.

--- COOK'S TIP ---
Starfruit is sometimes called carambola, and papayas may also be called paw paws.

2 Sprinkle ⅔ cup of the remaining sugar over the fruit pieces in the pan. Add the remaining fruit and sprinkle with the remaining ⅔ cup sugar.

3 Cover the pan and cook the fruit over medium-low heat until the sugar dissolves completely, 35–45 minutes. Shake the pan occasionally, but do not stir or the fruit will collapse.

4 Uncover the pan and simmer until the fruit begins to appear translucent, about 10 minutes. Remove the pan from the heat and let stand to cool.

5 Transfer the fruit and syrup to a serving bowl, then cover the bowl and chill overnight.

Iced Macaroon Cream with Raspberry Sauce

INGREDIENTS

Serves 6–8

3⅔ cups whipping cream
4 tbsp brandy or orange juice
2 tbsp sugar
12 crisp almond macaroons (about 4oz), coarsely crushed
raspberries, to decorate
1 cup raspberry sauce, to serve

COOK'S TIP

To make a quick raspberry sauce, purée about 8oz fresh raspberries, then push the purée through a nylon strainer to remove the pips and then sweeten to taste with confectioner's sugar.

1 Put the cream in a large bowl, preferably chilled, and whip until it starts to thicken.

2 Add the brandy or orange juice and sugar. Continue whipping until the cream will hold stiff peaks.

3 Add the macaroons and fold evenly into the cream.

4 Spoon into six or eight ramekins, or a 5 cup smooth-sided mold. Press in evenly to be sure there are no air pockets. Smooth the surface. Cover and freeze until firm. (Do not freeze longer than 1 day.)

5 To serve, dip the molds in hot water for 5–10 seconds, then invert on to a serving plate. Lift off the molds. Chill the desserts for 15–20 minutes to soften slightly.

6 Decorate with raspberries and serve with the sauce.

VARIATIONS

You could use coarsely broken meringue nests instead of crushed macaroons. Use almond liqueur instead of the brandy or orange juice.

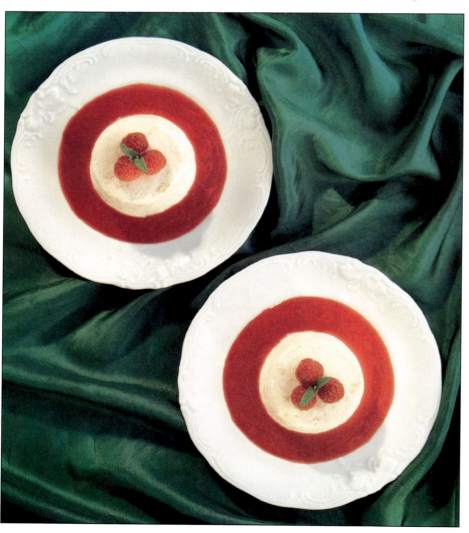

Raspberry Trifle

INGREDIENTS

Serves 6 or more

6 cups/1in cubes of spongecake or coarsely crumbled ladyfingers
4 tbsp medium sherry
4oz raspberry jelly
10oz raspberries
2 cups custard, flavored with 2 tbsp medium or sweet sherry
1½ cups sweetened whipped cream
toasted flaked almonds and mint leaves, to decorate

1 Spread half of the spongecake cubes or the coarsely crumbled ladyfingers over the bottom of a large serving bowl. (A glass bowl is best for presentation.)

2 Sprinkle half of the sherry over the cake to moisten it. Spoon over half of the jelly, dotting it evenly over the cake cubes.

3 Reserve a few raspberries for decoration. Make a layer of half of the remaining raspberries on top.

4 Pour over half of the custard, covering the fruit and cake cubes. Repeat the layers. Cover and chill for at least 2 hours.

---- VARIATION ----
Use other ripe fruit in the trifle such as apricots, peaches, nectarines, strawberries, with jelly and liqueur to suit.

5 Before serving, spoon the sweetened whipped cream evenly over the top. To decorate, sprinkle with toasted flaked almonds and arrange the reserved raspberries and the mint leaves on the top.

Fruity Ricotta Creams

Ricotta is an Italian soft cheese with a smooth texture and a mild, slightly sweet flavor. Served here with candied fruit peel and delicious semisweet chocolate, it is quite irresistible.

INGREDIENTS

Serves 4

1½ cups ricotta
2–3 tbsp Cointreau or other orange liqueur
2 tsp grated lemon rind
2 tbsp confectioner's sugar
⅔ cup heavy cream
5oz candied peel, such as orange, lemon and citron, finely chopped
2oz semisweet chocolate, finely chopped
chocolate curls, to decorate
amaretti cookies, to serve (optional)

1 Using the back of a wooden spoon, push the ricotta through a fine strainer into a large bowl.

2 Add the liqueur, lemon rind and sugar to the ricotta and beat well until the mixture is light and smooth.

3 Whip the cream in a large bowl until it forms soft peaks.

4 Gently fold the cream into the ricotta mixture with the candied peel and chopped chocolate.

5 Spoon the mixture into four glass serving dishes and chill for about 1 hour. Decorate the ricotta creams with chocolate curls and serve with amaretti cookies, if you like.

Hot Fruit with Maple Butter

INGREDIENTS

Serves 4

1 large mango
1 large papaya
1 small pineapple
2 bananas
½ cup unsalted butter
4 tbsp pure maple syrup
ground cinnamon, for sprinkling

1 Peel the mango and cut the flesh into large pieces. Halve the papaya and scoop out the seeds. Cut into thick slices, then peel away the skin.

2 Peel and core the pineapple and slice into thin wedges. Peel the bananas then halve them lengthwise.

3 Cut the butter into small dice and place in a food processor with the maple syrup, then process until the mixture is smooth and creamy.

4 Place the mango, papaya, pineapple and banana on a broiling rack and brush with the maple syrup butter.

5 Cook the fruit under a medium heat for about 10 minutes, until just tender, turning the fruit occasionally and brushing it with the butter.

6 Arrange the fruit on a warmed serving platter and dot with the remaining butter. Sprinkle over a little ground cinnamon and serve the fruit piping hot.

COOK'S TIP

Prepare the fruit just before broiling so it won't discolor. Check the label when buying maple syrup to make sure that it is 100% pure as imitations have little of the taste of the real thing.

Index

Almonds: almond syrup tart, 61
   sweet almond tart, 57
Amaretti: Amaretto soufflé, 22
   coffee jellies with amaretti cream, 50
Apples: apple brown Betty, 15
   apple pie, 70
   apple soufflé omelette, 81
   apple strudel, 24
   baked apples with apricots, 76
   chocolate fruit fondue, 24
   Eve's pudding, 14
Apricots: apricot and orange jelly, 40
   apricot mousse, 46
   apricots in Marsala, 86
   apricots with orange cream, 44
   baked apples with apricots, 76
Australian hazelnut pavlova, 33

Bananas: banana and passionfruit whip, 50
   banana cream pie, 73
   chocolate fruit fondue, 24
   coffee fudge sundaes, 47
   hot fruit with maple butter, 94
   hot spiced bananas, 84
   Thai fried bananas, 20
Batter: spiced Mexican fritters, 20
Blackcurrants: Russian fruit compôte, 78
Blueberries: blueberry pancakes, 80
   blueberry pie, 69
   pear and blueberry pie, 68
Brandy snaps: lemon cheesecake on brandy snaps, 37
Bread: Creole bread and butter pudding, 17
   summer fruit dessert, 34
Breadcrumbs: almond syrup tart, 61
   apple brown Betty, 15
   queen of puddings, 13

Candied fruit dessert, 14
Candied peel: fruity ricotta creams, 94
Cheesecake: banana cream pie, 73
   lemon cheesecake on brandy snaps, 37
Cherries jubilee, 86
Chestnuts: chocolate chestnut roulade, 52
Chocolate: chocolate chestnut roulade, 52
   chocolate fruit fondue, 24
   coffee fudge sundaes, 47
   chocolate mold, 32
   coffee, vanilla and chocolate stripe, 38
   Mississippi mud pie, 72
   white chocolate parfait, 48
Cider: spiced pears in cider, 77
Cinnamon: cinnamon and coconut rice, 12
   tropical fruits in cinnamon syrup, 90
Coconut: cinnamon and coconut rice, 12
   Thai fried bananas, 20
   white chocolate parfait, 48
Coffee: coffee fudge sundaes, 47
   coffee jellies with amaretti cream, 50
   coffee, vanilla and chocolate stripe, 38
Compôtes: Russian fruit compôte, 78
   warm autumn compôte, 82
Cream cheese: banana cream pie, 73
Creole bread and butter pudding, 17

Crêpes Suzette, 18

Dried fruit: apricot mousse, 46
   candied fruit dessert, 14
   Creole bread and butter pudding, 17
   fruit and rice ring, 42

Eggs: apple soufflé omelette, 81
Eve's pudding, 14

Figs: Greek fig and honey dessert, 78
   warm autumn compôte, 82
Fondue: chocolate fruit fondue, 24
Fools: orange and lemon fool
   rhubarb and orange fool, 44
Fritters: spiced Mexican fritters, 20
Fruit: chocolate fruit fondue, 24
   fruit and rice ring, 42
   fruit kabobs with mango-yogurt sauce, 90
   fruity ricotta creams, 94
   Greek fig and honey dessert, 78
   hot fruit with maple butter, 94
   Russian fruit compôte, 78
   summer fruit pudding, 34
   summer fruit trifle, 30
   tropical fruits in cinnamon syrup, 90
   warm autumn compôte, 82
Fudge: coffee fudge sundaes, 47

Gooseberry cream, 28
Grapes: chocolate fruit fondue, 24
Greek fig and honey dessert, 78

Hazelnuts: Australian hazelnut pavlova, 33
Honey: Greek fig and honey dessert, 78
   raspberry-honey cream, 30
Honeycomb mold, 29

Ice cream: cherries jubilee, 86
   coffee fudge sundaes, 47
Iced macaroon cream with raspberry sauce, 92

Jelly: apricot and orange jelly, 40
   coffee jellies with Amaretti cream, 50

Kabobs: fruit kabobs with mango-yogurt sauce, 90
Kiwis: chocolate fruit fondue, 24
   fruit kabobs with mango-yogurt sauce, 90

Lemons: honeycomb mold, 29
   lemon cheesecake on brandy snaps, 37
   surprise lemon dessert, 19
   warm lemon and syrup cake, 23

Macaroons: iced macaroon cream with raspberry sauce, 92
Mangoes: fruit kabobs with mango-yogurt sauce, 90
   hot fruit with maple butter, 94
   mango sorbet, 89
   tropical fruits in cinnamon syrup, 90
Meringue: Australian hazelnut pavlova, 33
   strawberry cream, 36

Mississippi mud pie, 72
Mississippi pecan pie, 64
Mousses: apricot mousse, 46
   ruby plum mousse, 82

Nectarines: chocolate fruit fondue, 24
Nuts: Australian hazelnut pavlova, 33
   chocolate chestnut roulade, 52
   Mississippi pecan pie, 64
   peanut butter tart, 62
   sweet almond tart,
   walnut and pear lattice pie, 65

Oatmeal: treacle and oatmeal tart, 66
Omelette: apple soufflé omelette, 81
Orange and lemon fool, 40
Oranges: apricots with orange cream, 44
   crêpe Suzette, 18
   fruit and rice ring, 42
   oranges with spiced cream, 66
   orange and lemon fool, 40
   rhubarb and orange fool, 44

Pancakes: blueberry pancakes, 80
   crêpes Suzette, 18
Papayas: hot fruit with maple butter, 94
   tropical fruits in cinnamon syrup, 90
Parfait: white chocolate parfait, 48
Passionfruit: banana and passionfruit whip, 50
   raspberry and passionfruit swirls, 43
Pastry: almond syrup tart, 61
   apple pie, 70
   apple strudel, 24
   blueberry pie, 69
   Mississippi mud pie, 72
   Mississippi pecan pie, 64
   peanut butter tart, 66
   pear and blueberry pie, 68
   rhubarb pie, 58
   spiced pumpkin pie, 60
   sweet almond tart, 57
   treacle and oatmeal tart, 66
   walnut and pear lattice pie, 65
   Yorkshire curd tart, 56
Peaches: baked peaches with raspberry sauce, 85
   peach Melba, 34
Peanut butter tart, 62
Pears: pear and blueberry pie, 68
   spiced pears in cider, 77
   walnut and pear lattice pie, 65
   warm autumn compôte, 82
Pecan nuts: Mississippi pecan pie, 64
Pies: apple pie, 70
   banana cream pie, 73
   blueberry pie, 69
   Mississippi mud pie, 72
   Mississippi pecan pie, 64
   pear and blueberry pie, 68
   rhubarb pie, 58
   spiced pumpkin pie, 60
   walnut and pear lattice pie, 65
Pineapple: chocolate fruit fondue, 24
   fruit kabobs with mango-yogurt sauce, 90
   hot fruit with maple butter, 94

Plums: plum and port sorbet, 88
   ruby plum mousse, 82
Pumpkin: spiced pumpkin pie, 60

Queen of puddings, 13

Raspberries: baked peaches with raspberry sauce, 85
   iced macaroon cream with raspberry sauce, 92
   raspberry and passionfruit swirls, 43
   raspberry-honey cream, 30
   raspberry trifle, 93
   Russian fruit compôte, 78
   spiced Mexican fritters, 20
   warm autumn compôte, 82
Red currants: Russian fruit compôte, 78
Rhubarb: rhubarb and orange fool, 44
   rhubarb pie, 58
Rice: cinnamon and coconut rice, 12
   fruit and rice ring, 42
Ricotta: fruity ricotta creams, 94
Roulade: chocolate chestnut roulade, 52
Ruby plum mousse, 82
Russian fruit compôte, 78

Sorbets: mango sorbet, 89
   plum and port sorbet, 88
Soufflés: Amaretto soufflé, 22
   apple soufflé omelette, 81
Spiced Mexican fritters, 20
Spiced pears in cider, 77
Spiced pumpkin pie, 60
Starfruit: tropical fruits in cinnamon syrup, 90
Strawberries: chocolate fruit fondue, 24
   fruit kabobs with mango-yogurt sauce, 90
   strawberry cream, 36
Summer fruit dessert, 34
Sweet almond tart, 57
Syrup: almond syrup tart, 61
   hot fruit with maple butter, 94
   warm lemon and syrup cake, 23

Tarts: almond syrup tart, 61
   peanut butter tart, 62
   sweet almond tart, 57
   treacle and oatmeal tart, 66
   Yorkshire curd tart, 56
Thai fried bananas, 20
Treacle and oatmeal tart, 66
Trifle: raspberry trifle, 93
   summer fruit trifle, 30
Tropical fruits in cinnamon syrup, 90

Vanilla: coffee, vanilla and chocolate stripe, 38

Walnut and pear lattice pie, 65
Warm autumn compôte, 82
White choclate parfait, 48

Yogurt: fruit kabobs with mango-yogurt sauce, 90
   Greek fig and honey dessert, 78
Yorkshire curd tart, 56